MW00737840

"*Africa's Business Revolution* thinking about Africa and it from a business standpoint, but also a social and environmental one. A very compelling read, rich in practical insights on the 'why' as well as on the 'how.' A great encouragement to do more and a must-read for today's leaders."

—**ALAIN BEJJANI**, CEO, Majid Al Futtaim Group

"*Africa's Business Revolution* makes the strongest case yet for investing in Africa. The book shows not only that the long-term trends are powerfully in the continent's favor, but also that a rich prize awaits investors who are able to recast unmet needs as opportunities for growth."

—**HAKEEM BELO-OSAGIE**, Chairman, Metis Capital Partners

"A powerful and compelling guide that captures practical know-how for doing profitable and socially impactful business in Africa. Its unique findings portray Africa as the new frontier, thereby making the most of renewed optimism in Africa through its rich, challenging, and inspiring context. Doing business in Africa is for the discerning, imaginative, and bold executive. This book reaffirms my conviction that Africa is the best-kept secret for a profitable and fulfilling business enterprise."

—**ALIKO DANGOTE**, President and Chief Executive, Dangote Industries Limited

"Africa is a billion-person market on the cusp of transformative growth—yet until now little has been published on how global businesses can be part of this exciting story. *Africa's Business Revolution* fills that gap: it weaves together the authors' rich experience with the perspectives of some of Africa's most successful business leaders."

—**MO IBRAHIM**, Founder and Chairman, Mo Ibrahim Foundation

"*Africa's Business Revolution* is a thought-provoking read that confronts many of the myths about Africa and provides a strategic guide to navigating an incredibly dynamic and diverse continent. Africa is experiencing a historic demographic change and I cannot think of a more opportune time for us all to consider the possibilities arising from this transformation."

—**CHRISTINE LAGARDE**, Managing Director,
International Monetary Fund

"Digitization is creating breakthrough opportunities not just to build businesses but to change millions of lives in Africa. More than most books on the subject, *Africa's Business Revolution* shows how companies can seize the opportunity, effect a paradigm shift—and do well by doing good across the continent."

—**PHUTHUMA NHLEKO**, Chairman, MTN Group

"This is an important and timely book that brings the scope and scale of Africa's exciting business opportunities alive for readers around the globe. *Africa's Business Revolution* is engaging, filled with vivid case studies, crisp analysis, and thoughtful insights on how to build strong local partnerships. This is a must-read for any global business leader looking for opportunities to deliver outsize returns to stakeholders while also meeting Africa's huge unmet demand for goods and services."

—**PENNY PRITZKER**, Founder and Chairman, PSP Partners;
former United States Secretary of Commerce

"The last great emerging market is Africa. For those investors interested in learning why the market offers enormous opportunities over the coming decade, *Africa's Business Revolution* is an indispensable guidebook."

—**DAVID M. RUBENSTEIN**, Co-Founder and
Co-Executive Chairman, The Carlyle Group

"Africa is not a special continent sitting on a different planet. It presents huge opportunities here and now, and many companies and entrepreneurs are already going after them successfully. This book is a major step in the normalization of the way the business world looks at and thinks about Africa. A must-read for business leaders."

—**TIDJANE THIAM**, CEO, Credit Suisse

AFRICA'S BUSINESS REVOLUTION

AFRICA'S BUSINESS REVOLUTION

HOW TO SUCCEED IN THE WORLD'S NEXT BIG GROWTH MARKET

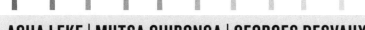

ACHA LEKE | MUTSA CHIRONGA | GEORGES DESVAUX

HARVARD BUSINESS REVIEW PRESS

Boston, Massachusetts

Copyright 2020 McKinsey & Company
All rights reserved
Printed in the United Kingdom by TJ International Ltd

10 9 8 7 6 5 4 3 2 1

No part of this publication may be reproduced, stored in or introduced into a retrieval system, or transmitted, in any form, or by any means (electronic, mechanical, photocopying, recording, or otherwise), without the prior permission of the publisher. Requests for permission should be directed to permissions@harvardbusiness.org, or mailed to Permissions, Harvard Business School Publishing, 60 Harvard Way, Boston, Massachusetts 02163.

The web addresses referenced in this book were live and correct at the time of the book's publication but may be subject to change.

Library of Congress Cataloging-in-Publication Data is forthcoming

ISBN: 9781633699984

From Acha

To all those who are building and growing businesses across the continent, creating jobs, delivering value for their shareholders, and making a difference in people's lives—this book is for you. I hope it inspires others to do the same.

From Mutsa

To all the entrepreneurs building businesses in Africa, however large or small—we're only getting started!

From Georges

To my family—Pascale, Audrey, Agathe, and Eleonore—and to all the young Africans and Asians who, like you, embrace global diversity and want to make a difference.

CONTENTS

PREFACE

As global business interest in Africa has blossomed, we have found ourselves traveling the world to help executives understand where the true opportunity lies, and how their businesses can seize that opportunity before their competitors do. A few years back, one of us (Acha) found himself in Seoul, presenting to the chairman of one of the largest Korean conglomerates. At that stage, the company had almost no presence in Africa and its executives were concerned that their Chinese competitors were stealing a march on them.

As always, the McKinsey team arrived at the meeting armed with a PowerPoint presentation, the first page of which was a map of Africa. We'd intended to flip quickly past it, but the chairman stopped us in our tracks. "You've made a mistake," he exclaimed. "You have two countries called Congo!" In fact, there *are* two countries named after the mighty River Congo. One is the mineral-rich but conflict-ridden Democratic Republic of the Congo (DRC), with a population of around eighty-seven million and a land area eighty times that of Belgium, its former colonial power. On the other side of the river is the Republic of the Congo, with a population of just 5 million but a GDP per capita ten times that of its neighbor, reflecting its position as a significant oil producer.

"Yes, there are two Congos. Why not? There are two Koreas!" we told the chairman. There were laughs all round, but this

FIGURE P-1

Africa's 54 countries are home to 1.2 billion people

African countries by population in 2017,
millions of people   ■ <10   ■ 10–40   ■ >40

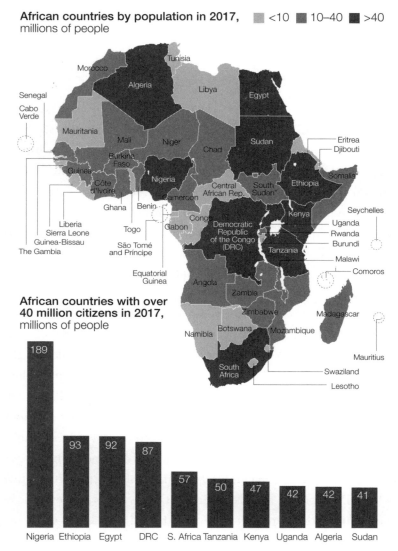

African countries with over
40 million citizens in 2017,
millions of people

Nigeria	Ethiopia	Egypt	DRC	S. Africa	Tanzania	Kenya	Uganda	Algeria	Sudan
189	93	92	87	57	50	47	42	42	41

*Data for Somalia and South Sudan from the World Bank. Other country data on map
came from the UN.

Source: United Nations World Population Prospects; World Bank; International Monetary
Fund; World Economic Outlook Database, April 2017.

moment of confusion underlined a real issue facing any company seeking to build or grow a business in Africa—how to navigate the continent's bewildering scale and complexity. Africa has fifty-four countries with a combined population of 1.2 billion (figure P-1). It has over a thousand languages and huge diversity in income levels, resource endowment, infrastructure development, educational attainment, and business sophistication.

It's one thing to get a handle on the physical map of Africa, but it's an even greater challenge to create an accurate mental map of the continent. In our experience, the instinct of most businesspeople is to underestimate Africa's size and potential as a market, and overestimate the challenges of doing business there.

Let's test your own perceptions: How many companies in Africa earn annual revenues of $1 billion or more? Take a guess.

If you guessed fewer than fifty such firms, you're in good company. We surveyed over a thousand business executives across Africa and the world, and fifty was the maximum number chosen by most respondents. Several said "zero." When we asked the same question at events such as the World Economic Forum, participants were only slightly more optimistic: most put the number of billion-dollar firms at between fifty and one hundred. The reality? There are *four hundred* such companies—and they are on average both faster-growing and more profitable than their global peers.[1] Africa's banks, for example, grew their revenues at double the global average between 2012 and 2017—and on average were more than twice as profitable as those in developed markets in 2017.[2]

You might need to reset your mental map of Africa in other ways too. Perhaps you see it as a continent of villages and smallholders; in fact, it will soon be the fastest-urbanizing region in the world. Africa already has as many cities with more than one million inhabitants as North America does, and more than 80 percent of its population growth over the next two decades will occur in cities. The income per capita of Africa's cities is more than double the continental average, making them attractive markets for many businesses.

How about technology? Like many observers, you might assume that Africa lags the world. But the reality is that this young continent, with a median age of around twenty, is an eager adopter and innovator in all things digital and mobile. There are already 122 million active users of mobile financial services in Africa.[3] The number of smartphone connections is forecast to double from 315 million in 2015 to 636 million in 2022—twice the projected number in North America and not far from the total in Europe.[4] Over the same period, mobile data traffic across Africa is expected to increase sevenfold.[5]

Why are our mental maps of Africa so faulty? In part, it's because so much of the news about Africa is negative. In a single week in 2017, for example, the *New York Times* ran the following articles: a profile of four boys from a village in Nigeria who had been abducted by Boko Haram; a report on the drowning deaths of migrants from Senegal in their desperate attempts to reach Europe; a new story on corruption in Angola; another on corruption in Tunisia; and a report on alleged government-sanctioned killings in the Democratic Republic of Congo. Is it any wonder that executives from developed countries may have skewed notions of what the environment is really like in Africa?

All of those stories were accurate and important to report, but such coverage needs to be balanced with other sources of information to gain a full picture of the actual conditions a business might face. Consider the following: While media accounts lead to a perception of widespread conflict, Africa has in fact become steadily more peaceful since 2000.[6] Armed conflicts persist, but there are fewer of them and they are more contained. Africa is often seen as synonymous with poverty, yet the share of Africans who are poor fell from 56 percent in 1990 to 43 percent in 2012, according to the World Bank.[7] Adult literacy rates have climbed by ten percentage points since 1990 to 63 percent—still too low but improving rapidly; and again, wide variations exist across Africa.[8] Health is also improving, with life expectancies rising and infant mortality falling.

We've written this book in part to help leaders everywhere draw a more accurate mental map of the continent—the first critical step to seizing the opportunities for building profitable, sustainable businesses there.

WHAT YOU WILL GET FROM THIS BOOK

The idea for this book was sparked by a challenge from Harvard Business Review Press, who told us there was a need for a comprehensive book on the African business opportunity by people with deep experience in the continent. We leaped at the chance, and immediately began distilling the insights from over three thousand McKinsey consulting engagements across Africa over the past twenty years. We drew on our extensive research library—including the McKinsey Global Institute's *Lions on the Move* reports on Africa's economic progress, as well as studies on digitization, job creation, the African consumer, the continent's electricity sector, and women's advancement.[9] We commissioned the executive survey mentioned earlier, gauging the views of over one thousand business practitioners in every region of the world. Most importantly, we interviewed dozens of successful CEOs and entrepreneurs, as well as leaders of major development institutions, to learn from their own stories of the peaks and pitfalls of business building in Africa.

One such business builder is Nigeria-based Aliko Dangote. Of all the executives we asked, he was the only one to guess correctly that Africa has four hundred billion-dollar companies. Perhaps that is testimony to his confidence in Africa's business prospects and the boldness of his own growth vision. From a trading company started with a small loan from his uncle in 1978, Dangote has built one of Africa's largest industrial firms, which manufactures commodities including cement, sugar, and flour in massive volumes. By 2017, the Dangote Group's annual revenues exceeded $4 billion, and Dangote had become Africa's richest person and the world's richest black man. Yet he continued to aim high. His new growth projects include the world's largest single-train petroleum refinery, scheduled to open at the end of 2019. It is being built near Lagos, Nigeria's bustling commercial capital, at cost of $12 billion.[10] Dangote's philosophy is: "Think big, dream big, and do big things."[11]

This book tells the stories of many companies that are thinking big in Africa. Some are African-born champions like Dangote, Kenya's Equity Bank, and South Africa–based mobile telecoms operator MTN. Others are global multinationals like Coca-Cola, GE, and Total. Several are startups that are bringing together global and African expertise and investment to build fast-growing businesses in new industries. One example is Jumia, one of the continent's leading e-commerce players. Another is M-Kopa, which has sold off-grid solar-power kits to six hundred thousand rural households, and financed them via mobile money.

Though these companies differ widely in their geographic and sector focus, what they have in common is the imagination to see Africa's unmet needs as opportunities for entrepreneurship, and the long-term commitment required to build businesses of meaningful scale. Although each is a commercially successful enterprise, their innovations and investments have also created real social impact by connecting people to services that were previously unavailable, boosting productivity and growth, and creating large numbers of jobs.

Indeed, the fastest-growing and most profitable businesses in Africa typically see challenges as a spur for innovation and unmet market demand as room for growth. For example, Africa faces huge gaps in education, health systems, electric power, and transport infrastructure and lags in global ease-of-doing-business rankings. These issues might scare off the fainthearted, but they make Africa a fertile arena for entrepreneurs.

It is for such entrepreneurs, as well as executives seeking to expand their operations in Africa or access the market for the first time, that we have written this book.

In the first part, we set out to answer the question: *Why Africa, why now?* We challenge you to reset your mental map of Africa and take a fresh look at the opportunities presented by the continent's growing markets. We spell out how much room there is for businesses to grow, and we highlight the long-term trends and untapped opportunities you can harness to build a successful enterprise.

In part 2, we present a strategic guide to translating those opportunities into enduring business value—a guide that is just as relevant for Africa-born companies seeking to expand across the continent as it is for companies coming to Africa from other regions. We home in on four imperatives to win to Africa: choosing the right geographic portfolio, innovating your business model, building resilience and managing risks, and unleashing Africa's talent.

The purpose of this book, however, goes beyond creating value for shareholders: we want to show you not just how to profit from Africa's future, but also how to help shape it for the better. We are convinced that business has a profound role to play in accelerating Africa's development and enabling its people to live better, more fulfilling lives. This is truly a continent where businesses can do well by doing good—whether by connecting people with technology, supplying a wider choice of manufactured goods at lower prices, helping build expanding cities and vital infrastructure, or nurturing skills for a young and fast-growing workforce.

———————

Is now the right time to build a business in Africa? For all three of us, that question has been a very personal one. Acha and Mutsa left behind promising careers in the West, returning home to Africa to pursue the uncertain but passion-imbued task of building McKinsey's practice here. Georges left Asia to do the same. We're thrilled to be part of Africa's exciting story of business and economic growth. We hope this book inspires you to join us.

PART ONE

WHY AFRICA, WHY NOW?

CHAPTER 1

A GIANT AWAKES

One of our objectives in writing this book is to prompt business executives and entrepreneurs from the Americas, Asia-Pacific, Europe, and the Middle East to take a fresh look at the business opportunities in Africa—and while you're at it, to spend some time exploring our beautiful continent. One must-do activity is a game drive in one of Africa's remarkable nature reserves—perhaps the Serengeti in Tanzania, Kruger National Park in South Africa, or Namibia's Etosha National Park. As you bump along the rutted savannah on the back of a Land Rover, however, you'll discover that some of Africa's most magnificent animals can be hard to spot. A leopard, for example, might be perched still and silent on the branch of a marula tree, its coat a natural camouflage under the dappled shadows of the leaves. The untrained eye is likely to see only the tree; but those who know what they're looking for will pick out the leopard a mile away.

That's a fair analogy for the business world. Executives with on-the-ground experience in Africa sometimes manage to spot opportunities that are hidden from the view of global observers. Just look at the story of SABMiller. The beer maker started as South Africa's national champion, snapped up global brands such as Pilsner Urquell, Miller Lite, and Peroni, and ended up on the London Stock Exchange's FTSE 100 list before being acquired by rival Anheuser-Busch InBev for $103 billion in late 2016. It was SABMiller's success across the African continent, along with its operations in Latin America, that made it such a growth star and justified the eye-watering price tag for its takeover.

From 2007 to 2016, the brewer saw its African sales outside of South Africa climb from $280 million to $1 billion. By 2016, SABMiller had brewing operations in around forty of Africa's fifty-four countries. Mark Bowman was the managing director of SABMiller's Africa region during that decade. He told us, "We spotted a huge opportunity in Africa's beer market, and we seized it at the right moment. In the early part of this century, most global firms saw Africa as unattractive, so we had limited competition."

SABMiller knew otherwise. The continent's population was growing by around 2.5 percent a year, much faster than most other regions. Seventy percent of the population was under the age of thirty, most countries were increasingly urban, and their economies were growing—all bullish signs for beer consumption. SABMiller's insight was simple yet powerful: like consumers the world over, Africans like beer. When they can start spending a portion of earnings on nonessentials, one of the first luxuries they turn to is an upgrade from home brews to commercial brands. "We realized that, if we acted early, we could become number one or two in many African markets," Bowman said. "We recognized that if we established a leading position, even if it was small in the beginning, it could grow into quite a big business. Even so, I don't think we ever fully appreciated that African markets would generate the value that they did."

SABMiller began acquiring existing African breweries in 1993, starting with a 50 percent stake in a money-losing operation in Tanzania. With its local partners, it quickly turned that brewery around, tripling production and generating healthy profits within three years. That whetted its appetite for more. "We more or less tried to buy anything that was for sale, had a reasonable brand and had reasonable prospects," recalls Bowman. He says the deals were often complex, burdened by poor bookkeeping and questionable tax-avoidance schemes practiced by the acquired breweries, but SABMiller pushed ahead as long as there was some prospect of generating a positive return. "With hindsight, what we thought was expensive was actually cheap," he says.

The company started with a conservative strategy, using secondhand equipment in its new breweries to save money and cycling in end-of-career executives to manage them. Bowman recounts, "As we developed confidence in the business, Africa became a much bigger priority. We completely transformed our philosophy and approach and developed a much bolder long-term vision of what Africa could deliver." One element of that new strategy was an aggressive program of brewery building across the continent. With its equipment-supplier partners, SABMiller developed a standardized "brewery in a box" that it could quickly assemble. A second element was to hone its marketing insights: using the brand-positioning approach it had developed globally, SABMiller created a diverse portfolio of African brands tailored to local markets.

In Nigeria, for example, SABMiller developed a new brand, Hero. "Our head of marketing in Nigeria convinced us that this was the right name, because people saw themselves as everyday heroes, heroes of their own story," Bowman told us. SABMiller wanted the new beer to come across as local, not the product of a multinational. It designed the label with a rising sun, a favorite symbol of the Igbo people, an ethnic group native to Nigeria. And in a country where it can take up to six hours to earn enough to buy a half-liter of beer, SABMiller priced the brew 25 percent below the market-leading Star brand. Bowman recounts the launch of the Hero brewery, an event attended by Nigeria's then-president, among other luminaries. "Three or four distributors came up to me and told me the history of the Hero brand—even though it was totally new! They'd completely bought it in their minds. It turned out to be one of the most successful brands we ever launched, and our production was never able to keep up with demand."

SABMiller's approach to brands also took into account the huge differences in spending power among African consumers. By the time it was acquired by Anheuser-Busch InBev in 2016, SABMiller had begun to extend its portfolio beyond its traditional mainstream beer offering. In its drive to appeal to low-income consumers, it acquired a small brewery in Zambia that specialized in a commercial version of the local home brew made with sorghum and maize. SABMiller would eventually market the brew as Shake Shake (you really do have to shake the brew before drinking because of the sediment) in a dozen countries. At the same time, SABMiller also made a strong play for consumers higher up the income pyramid. It launched Castle Lite, a South African beer brand, in multiple African markets, targeted at "upper mainstream" consumers at a price premium. "We were spectacularly successful with Castle Lite," Bowman said. "The consumer proposition was very strong and simple: an ice-cold reward that is much healthier and better for you."

As Bowman reminded us, though, it takes more than a smart strategy to succeed in Africa. Underpinning SABMiller's growth was a mindset of winning: "Right from the beginning, our people had a can-do attitude. They just went out there and built the business. They were the real heroes of this story."

In 2011, we published an article in *Harvard Business Review* entitled "Cracking the Next Growth Market: Africa." We posited Africa was one of the world's fastest-growing regions, and that farsighted companies able to spot the African opportunity and act on it before others would reap enormous gains. SABMiller's story is a perfect example. Today, we believe the long-term growth prospects for Africa are even greater—and the case for businesses to invest in the continent is even more compelling.

We don't pretend that Africa is an easy place to do business, given its geographic complexity, infrastructure gaps, and relative economic and political volatility. Despite these challenges, we believe that companies and investors in every part of the world should be taking a close look at Africa today and its place in their growth strategy for the next twenty years. Here are four good reasons:

- Africa is a 1.2 billion–person market in the midst of an historic economic acceleration.

- Hundreds of large companies, home-grown and multinational, have already built successful businesses in Africa, but there is room for many more.

- Africa has huge unfulfilled demand, making it ripe for entrepreneurship and innovation at scale.

- You can achieve extraordinary growth and profitability—provided you get your strategy and execution right.

A 1.2 BILLION-PERSON MARKET ON THE CUSP OF TRANSFORMATIVE GROWTH

Africa is a big place: its land area is second only to Asia's, and it contains a major share of the world's agricultural land and mineral reserves. Its current population of around 1.2 billion is projected to double over the next thirty years, making Africa an exception in a world of slowing population growth. Those numbers should be reason enough to interest global businesses.

What really makes it a continent to watch, though, is the historic economic shift under way. A glance at world economic history gives an indication of what could be ahead for Africa. In Europe and North America, for example, average per capita income barely increased for almost two thousand years, but suddenly soared with the Industrial Revolution, increasing twentyfold between 1820 and 2015.[1] Asia's boom came later but was much faster: its GDP per capita increased tenfold between 1960 and 2015. And within Asia, China's rise in per capita income has been even more dramatic: it took just three decades for GDP per capita to multiply tenfold after the launch of economic reforms at the end of the 1970s.

One of us (Georges) spent seven years in China at the height of its economic acceleration. Many African cities today remind him of Chinese cities such as Chongqing or Wuhan twenty years ago: they have the same hustle, the same entrepreneurial energy, and a similar emerging class of aspiring citizens. The urban energy of Lagos, Nairobi, or Abidjan today suggests that much of Africa has reached an inflection point where a sufficiently large pool of people have risen beyond providing for their basic needs and have the wherewithal to discriminate among consumer goods, save for their first washing machine or refrigerator, or send their kids to better schools. Indeed, in many parts of urban Africa, there are signs that the simultaneous increases in population and per capita income are triggering exponential growth in demand. That is reflected in the proliferation of retail outlets, cell phone networks, restaurants, housing developments, car dealerships—and traffic jams.

Tidjane Thiam, the Ivorian-born CEO of Credit Suisse and former head of Prudential, the global insurer, is a keen observer of this growth phenomenon—and its implications for business. "The human brain thinks in a linear fashion," he remarked to us, "but exponential growth is in fact more common in nature. Think of an acorn growing into an oak tree." Thiam gained firsthand experience of this truth while building Prudential's business in emerging Asia. One $50 million investment multiplied to $4 billion in little over 15 years—an eightyfold expansion. Thiam believes that conditions in many African markets today offer similar opportunities. "You've got the demographic boom combined with GDP growth rates of 6, 7, or 8 percent." Companies that get in early and shape the right strategy can sustain double-digit profit growth over decades, he said. "There is an element of breaking ground, but the long-term rewards will be very high."

The numbers suggest that Africa is in the midst of a significant acceleration (see figure 1-1). Real GDP grew at an average annual rate of little over 2 percent during the 1980s and 1990s, but then leaped ahead to 5.4 percent in 2000–2010, making Africa the world's second-fastest-growing region after emerging Asia. Notably, this growth spurt was driven in nearly equal measures by labor-force growth and productivity growth, marking the end of a long period of stagnant productivity. In the late 1990s, private capital flows to Africa (including foreign direct investment, equity, and debt) overtook aid inflows and remittances for the first time in decades.

FIGURE 1-1

The numbers highlight Africa's acceleration—and the opportunity for business

5.6

trillion dollars in projected consumer and business spending by 2025

1.2

billion people—with population expected to double by 2050

11

million square miles of land—three times that of Europe

400

companies with annual revenues of $1 billion or more

122

million active users of mobile financial services

89

cities of over 1 million inhabitants by 2030

54

countries expected to create the world's largest free trade area

2x

potential growth in manufacturing output by 2025

Rising productivity and investment in the first decade of the twenty-first century reflected the increasing diversification of Africa's economies away from resources exports. Although Africa benefited from soaring global demand for oil and minerals during this period, commodities explain only part of the continent's growth over that decade. McKinsey's 2010 report, *Lions on the Move*, found that oil and natural resources accounted directly or indirectly for just 24 percent of Africa's GDP growth from 2000 through to 2008.[2] Other sectors accounted for most of the growth surge: tourism, financial services, transport, telecommunications, and construction all grew at annual rates of around 8 percent over this period. GDP grew rapidly both in countries with significant resource exports (5.4 percent) and in those without (4.6 percent).

After this heady decade, Africa's growth slowed sharply— to an annual rate of 3.3 percent between 2010 and 2015. This was prompted by the twin shocks of the Arab Spring, which halted growth altogether in Egypt, Libya, and Tunisia; and the collapse of oil prices, which caused growth to fall sharply in oil-exporting countries including Algeria, Angola, and Nigeria. In the rest of Africa, however, real annual GDP growth grew from 4.1 percent in the period from 2000 to 2010 to 4.4 percent between 2010 and 2015.

No doubt, many African countries will remain vulnerable to economic and political volatility. In 2016–2017, for example, Nigeria suffered its first economic contraction in a quarter century as oil production slumped.[3] In the same period, South Africa's already slow growth was further hampered when its respected finance minister was fired and credit ratings agencies downgraded its sovereign debt. The slowdown in Africa's two largest economies was felt across the continent.

In early 2018, however, a change of president in South Africa reinvigorated investor confidence and sent the rand to a three-year high against the US dollar. Recovering oil prices and continuing economic diversification lifted Nigeria out of recession. Egypt's GDP growth was expected to reach 5 percent, while the World Bank forecast Ghana to be the world's fastest-growing economy in 2018.[4] Those developments were a reminder that, despite volatility, Africa's long-term growth prospects remain promising. Overall, GDP is still expanding faster than the world average and is forecast to accelerate to make Africa once again the world's second-fastest-growing region.

Of the over one thousand respondents in our executive survey, the majority concur with these forecasts, and predict that most African households will join the consumer class in the next twenty years. They also expect that rising investment in both digital technologies and natural resources—the new and old economies—will boost development. Nearly 90 percent of African-based companies, and 58 percent of those based in other regions, expect their revenues in Africa to grow over the next five years, and most plan to expand their African footprint to additional countries (figure 1-2).

Ordinary Africans are also strikingly optimistic about the future. For example, a McKinsey global citizen survey conducted in 2017 found that nearly two-thirds of Nigerians believed their country would be better for the next generation. In developed nations such as the United Kingdom, by contrast, 60 percent of respondents thought the next generation would be worse off.[5] That points to Africa's part in a "great rebalancing" of the global economy toward emerging markets.[6] As a 2017 *McKinsey Quarterly* article expressed it, "There are three geographic entities—India, China, and Africa—in which urbanization is empowering populations that exceed one billion people, and a

FIGURE 1-2

Most companies see Africa as a major growth market

Among respondents to our Africa business survey, Africa-based companies are especially bullish.

Of the following scenarios in Africa over the next 20 years, which do you believe are likely to occur? % of respondents*

| Africa's combined GDP is one of the fastest-growing in the world. | Most African households have joined the consumer class. | Africa's educational performance has improved significantly, due to digital technologies and other investments. | New investments in Africa's mineral resources have contributed significantly to the continent's economic growth. |

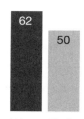

What changes do you expect for your organization in Africa in the next five years? % of respondents*

| Increase in number of countries where the organization operates | Increase in revenue from Africa | Increase in workforce size in Africa |

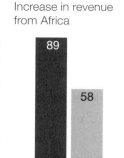

*Total respondents = 1,025 (respondents from Africa = 253; from all other regions = 772).

Source: Mckinsey Insights executive survey on business in Africa, 2017.

fourth, Southeast Asia, with more than half a billion. Together, these enormous 'ICASA' (India, China, Africa, and Southeast Asia) markets hold the potential for significant continued expansion. We expect more than roughly half of global growth over the next ten years to come from these geographies."[7]

Our colleagues point out that, of all the ICASA markets, Africa has the most unfilled potential. But it also faces the greatest challenges, including increasing sustainable urbanization, accelerating infrastructure development, and deepening regional integration. A failure to achieve any one of these could stall growth. In chapter 2, we look at these challenges and the role that business can play in solving them. For now, it's worth pointing out two efforts by African governments that are already making tangible economic impact, and that have the potential to create a sea change if they reach critical mass.

The first is a drive to improve the ease of doing business—an area in which Africa has long lagged other regions. Several African governments have introduced reforms such as setting maximum processing times for permits and registrations, increasing the transparency of government fee structures, and implementing risk-based compliance processes that focus effort on more probable contraventions. These efforts to make Africa more business friendly have begun to yield results. For example, Nigeria jumped twenty-four places in the World Bank's 2018 ease-of-doing-business ranking, from 169th to 145th, thanks to a reform effort that has put in place speedier business registration, improved efficiency in ports, and a new visa-on-arrival system for visitors. According to the World Bank, African countries implemented more than eighty reforms to the business environment in the year to June 2017, and four of the ten most improved countries worldwide, including Nigeria, were in Africa.[8]

Rwanda was several steps ahead of most other African nations, and is now a model for other efforts. In 2007, the East African nation set up a task force to improve its business environment. Reforms included setting up an effective "One Stop Center" for investors, streamlining construction permitting, introducing a simplified fixed fee for property registration, extending customs hours, and instituting risk-based customs inspections. Its ranking on the ease of doing business climbed from 150th in the world in 2008 to 32nd in 2014.[9]

The second notable effort is to remove trade and travel barriers between Africa's fifty-four countries to accelerate regional integration. African governments have been working for years to counter fragmentation by forming trading blocs that reduce tariffs and red tape for member countries. For example, the six-member East African Community and the fifteen-member Southern African Development Community have both seen their intra-bloc trade grow at around 15 percent a year over the past decade.[10] The integration of Africa's regional markets could soon accelerate. By 2017, twenty-two African countries had ratified membership of the Tripartite Free Trade Area, which will combine more than 600 million people in a single trading bloc, forming the thirteenth-largest economy in the world. In March 2018, forty-four countries agreed to establish the African Continental Free Trade Area. If ratified by all signatory countries, it will be the biggest trade agreement since the formation of the World Trade Organization in 1995.

The late Calestous Juma, professor of the Practice of International Development at Harvard's Kennedy School of Government, had long argued that larger markets would spur Africa's industrial development, including a shift to higher-value products. He noted, "This will not only create jobs but it will also have the added advantage of diversifying

Africa's economies. The associated technological development will lead to the creation of new industries."[11] We have confidence that the Continental Free Trade Area will become reality sooner rather than later, and prove him right. One encouraging sign is the move to visa-free travel between African countries. When McKinsey partnered with the African Development Bank and the World Economic Forum in 2012 to create the African Visa Openness Index, only five African nations offered visa-free or visa-on-arrival access to all fellow Africans. By 2018 that number had risen to close to twenty. Many of these countries have already seen sharp increases in the number of tourist arrivals and business visitors.

MORE BIG COMPANIES THAN YOU IMAGINED—BUT ROOM FOR MANY MORE

Some of the companies we feature in this book—like Coca-Cola, Comcraft, SABMiller, and Total—have been operating successful businesses in Africa for fifty or one hundred years. But many global companies only started to explore the continent's potential in the mid-1990s. McKinsey was one of them. Although we had worked in Africa since the 1970s, we opened our first office in Johannesburg in 1995—shortly after Nelson Mandela was elected as South Africa's first post-apartheid president. As we worked across dozens of countries and opened a further six offices across the continent, we found ourselves in the midst of an economic awakening in which business was playing a central part.

In those early years, just visiting clients was a challenge. Flights were so infrequent that it was faster to travel the three thousand miles from Yaoundé, Cameroon, to Dakar, Senegal, by way of Paris than trying to navigate through the airline schedules for hops across Africa. One of us (Mutsa) remembers arriving at one of the only business hotels in Lagos at 10 p.m. one Sunday night, and having to wait three hours to check in, as the hotel was full to capacity and accepted payment only in US cash. Today, there are dozens of hotels to choose from, many of international standard. Indeed, one manifestation of Africa's business boom has been the proliferation of international hotel brands and air travel routes.

Who are the executives you might meet in the marble-clad lobbies of one of these new hotels or on one of the many intra-continental flights? They could be from just about any sector: a manager from Shoprite, the South Africa–based supermarket chain that now operates more than twenty-five hundred stores across thirteen African countries; or an executive from one of Africa's many cross-border banks. Perhaps you might overhear a conversation between executives from France's Michelin and Côte d'Ivoire's SIFCA, which have partnered to build some of the world's largest rubber-production facilities in West Africa. There's every chance you'll bump into someone from MTN, the mobile phone company with more than 200 million subscribers in twenty-two nations in Africa and the Middle East.

In fact, MTN's growth story neatly mirrors the continent's: in 2000, the entire sub-Saharan African region had fewer tele-phone lines than the island of Manhattan alone. By 2016, there were more than 700 million mobile phone connections across the continent, roughly one for every adult. South Africa–based MTN increased its subscriber base thirty-two-fold in the first ten years after its founding in 1994.

The health sector has enjoyed an equally rapid accelera-tion, driven by urbanization and expansion of health systems. We expect that Africa's pharmaceutical market will be worth

$40 billion to $65 billion by 2020—double or triple its 2013 value.[12] Several large pharmaceutical companies are riding this wave. For example, South Africa–based Aspen Pharmacare, founded in 1997, built a presence in multiple African markets and is today a leading global generics player, with twenty-six facilities on six continents. Its 2016 revenues reached nearly $3 billion.[13]

Companies in the energy sector have grown fast too. Total, the France-based oil major, has nearly a century-long history in Africa—but it has capitalized on the continent's recent surge in demand for energy by expanding both its upstream oil and gas production and its downstream distribution network. As of 2017, it was pumping the equivalent of more than six hundred thousand barrels a day from Africa's abundant oil and gas resources—and selling much of it to African customers via its network of four thousand service stations, the continent's largest. "Our mission is to bring energy to our retail customers, and not only to produce the natural resources of these countries," Total's chairman and CEO, Patrick Pouyanné, told us. "Africa now represents 30 percent of our group's activity worldwide, and is a major long-term pillar of our growth."

In the transport and travel sector, consider the story of state-owned Ethiopian Airlines, which has driven an aggressive expansion strategy that nearly tripled its passenger numbers from 3.1 million in 2010 to 8.8 million in 2017. In the year to June 2017, the airline recorded a full-year profit of $232 million on revenues of $2.7 billion—more than many global airlines.[14] Today Ethiopian Airlines serves around ninety routes across Africa and beyond.[15] It is also the technical and strategic partner of Togo-based startup Asky Airlines, in which it holds a 40 percent stake. Asky itself, started on the initiative of several African governments and private-sector businesses in 2010, has addressed another gap: a lack of reliable air travel connections in Central and West Africa. It has grown rapidly and now serves twenty-three cities in the region.[16] (One of its routes is from Dakar to Yaoundé—so, thankfully, we no longer have to make that trip via Paris.)

These are just a few of the companies we've tracked via our database of large companies operating in Africa. That research has revealed surprising figures: four hundred companies earning revenues of $1 billion or more and nearly seven hundred companies with revenue greater than $500 million (figure 1-3). These companies are increasingly regional or pan-African.

FIGURE 1-3

Africa's 700 largest companies earn a combined $1.4 trillion in revenues

Breakdown of companies by revenue size, April 2016

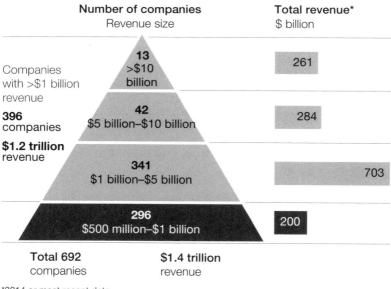

Total 692 companies

$1.4 trillion revenue

*2014 or most recent data.

Source: MGI African companies database; McKinsey Global Institute analysis.

They have grown faster than their peers in the rest of the world in local currency terms, and they are also more profitable than their global peers in most sectors.[17] Around two-fifths of them are publicly listed, and the remainder are privately held. Just over half are owned by Africa-based private shareholders, while 27 percent are foreign-based multinationals and 17 percent are state-owned enterprises.

In 2015, Africa's seven hundred largest companies together boasted $1.4 trillion in annual revenue. Seventy percent came from nonresource sectors such as retail, agri-processing, health care, financial services, manufacturing, and construction—evidence of the continent's progressive diversification.

Despite some notable corporate success stories, however, Africa lags behind other emerging regions in hosting large companies. Excluding South Africa, it has just 60 percent of the number one would expect if it were on a par with peer regions.[18] In fact, nearly half of Africa's big firms are based in South Africa (figure 1-4). Moreover, Africa's big companies are smaller, on average, than those in other emerging economies. The average large African corporation has annual revenue of $2.7 billion, compared with around $4 billion to $4.5 billion for big companies in Brazil, India, Malaysia, Mexico, and Russia, for instance. Outside South Africa, Africa's firms earn less than half the revenue of their emerging market peers as a proportion of GDP. No African company was featured in the 2017 global *Fortune* 500. By comparison, Brazil and India, whose GDPs are smaller than that of the African continent, each boasted seven companies on that list and China had 109.

Because of these twin issues—too few large firms and too little scale among those that do exist—the total revenue pool of large companies in Africa (excluding South Africa) is about a third of what it could be.[19] There also remains a high degree

FIGURE 1-4

Nearly half of Africa's big firms are based in South Africa

Companies with more than $500 million in revenue, by region, 2014,*
number of companies

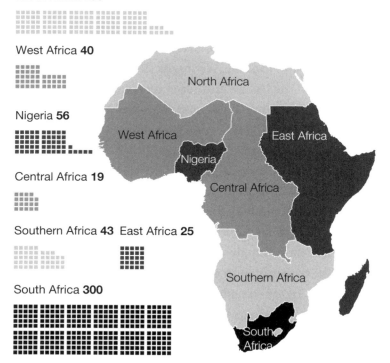

North Africa **133**

West Africa **40**

Nigeria **56**

Central Africa **19**

Southern Africa **43**   East Africa **25**

South Africa **300**

Regional share of Africa's total, %

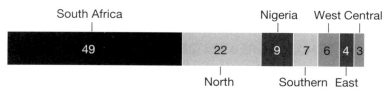

*Regional definition from the African Development Bank; 2014 or most recent data.

Note: Includes multinational corporations with local branches registered in Africa; does not include those based outside of Africa.

Source: MGI African companies database; McKinsey Global Institute analysis.

of fragmentation in many sectors, suggesting considerable unmet potential for companies to build scale. In the food and agri-processing sector, for example, the top three firms hold a combined market share of 25 percent or less in nearly all of Africa's largest economies.

Africa's relative lack of big companies matters not just for shareholders but for society, because these firms are the primary drivers of economic growth. We might think of big companies as the baobabs of the business landscape: not only do they tower above the rest, they also have deeper roots and longer life spans. Known as the tree of life, the baobab produces highly nutritious fruit that sustains many communities. Business baobabs, too, enliven their local economies: they contribute disproportionately to higher wages and taxes, productivity improvement, innovation, and technology dissemination. Like baobabs, large firms create their own ecosystems, fostering small-business creation through their supply chains and distribution networks. They are also better able to attract capital, which means they are much more likely to compete on the global stage. We put a forest of baobabs on the cover of this book because we believe Africa has the space—and need—not just for the hundreds of billion-dollar companies that are thriving across the continent today, but for many more.

UNMET DEMAND CREATES OPPORTUNITY FOR ENTREPRENEURS TO INNOVATE AT SCALE

Africa's vast unmet needs and unfulfilled demand make it a continent ripe for entrepreneurship and innovation at scale. And if it is to build its rightful number of large companies, then many of its younger firms will need to think big: they are the business baobabs of the future. Indeed, smaller and medium-sized companies have a critical role to play in accelerating economic development, serving the unmet needs of African markets, and especially creating jobs. The World Bank, for example, estimates that SMEs are responsible for 77 percent of all jobs in Africa, and as much as half of GDP in some countries. Midsized companies in particular are major job creators: McKinsey research shows that firms with between fifty and two hundred employees create jobs at twice the pace of both large corporations and small businesses.

In the course of writing this book, we encountered dozens of entrepreneurs who have launched startups explicitly targeted at addressing Africa's unmet demand. One of them is US-born Brooks Washington, founder of the Nairobi-based investment company Roha. He has made the development of greenfield manufacturing plants in Africa a core focus of his business. Washington told us that he has scoured the continent for opportunities where "we can build defensible businesses that match latent demand with global technology." One such opportunity is glass-bottle manufacturing in Ethiopia to supply the country's fast-growing beverage industry: to date, drinks makers have had to import 90 percent of their bottles. Roha has partnered with South Africa–based Consol Glass and the Development Bank of Ethiopia to build a $80 million glass-bottle plant in Debre Birhan, some seventy-five miles from Addis Ababa. When completed, the plant will have the capacity to produce 200 million bottles a year.

Another notable startup is Gro Intelligence, whose web application and tools provide a real-time picture of the factors influencing agricultural commodities, to clients in the financial services, physical trading, consulting, and sourcing and procurement sectors. It was launched in Kenya in 2014 by Sara

Menker, an Ethiopian-born former Wall Street commodities trader. Reflecting on the insights that led her to launch the company, she told us, "At the time in the US, land prices were skyrocketing. I said, 'Hold on. I come from a place that has a lot of land that's super-cheap. People are buying land in areas of the US at $15,000 an acre, but in Ethiopia I could get a hundred-year lease for $1 an acre. So I started looking at investing in agriculture in Africa."

But Menker soon realized there was a reason agricultural land was so cheap: farmers and investors lacked the information they needed to choose crops and markets, manage risks like weather, and identify where and when to invest in infrastructure. That gap led her to create Gro Intelligence, which she describes as "a Wikipedia for agriculture, but with a very deep analytical engine built on top of it." Its clients range from some of the world's largest sovereign wealth funds and hedge funds to individual commodity traders in Africa and around the globe. One coffee trader in Ethiopia who exports large quantities of coffee beans to Germany, using Gro Intelligence's online platform, learned that much of his coffee was being reexported to Eastern Europe, so he started exporting directly to Poland at higher margins. Menker's innovation is thus helping other African entrepreneurs build scale.

One of Africa's most ambitious startups is Jumia, launched in 2012 and today one of the continent's leading e-commerce companies. Its growth strategy, too, is targeted directly at addressing unmet demand. Sacha Poignonnec, Jumia's French-born co-CEO, told us: "In Africa, there is growing demand and a shortage of supply. Consumers lack choice and want a better shopping experience." He says this structural gap between supply and demand is visible on the ground in Nigeria, where there are millions of people with growing discretionary income but few formal retail stores per capita. "You also see it at global airports, where Africans are lined up with heavy luggage, full of products they cannot easily find back home."[20]

Poignonnec points out that in Africa, there are sixty thousand people per formal retail outlet—compared with just about four hundred people per store in the United States. Even in comparison with other developing regions such as Asia and Latin America, Africa is woefully underpenetrated in retail options. Though global and African retailers such as Carrefour and Shoprite are rapidly building new stores, Poignonnec believes that this expansion will not close the gap between supply and demand anytime soon. In part, this is because limited access to land and financing constrains the development of big-format retail in many African countries, and in part it is because traffic congestion in Africa's burgeoning cities simply makes it too hard for customers to get to malls.

By Jumia's calculations, online sales currently stand at just 0.5 percent of total retail sales in Africa—compared with 4 percent in India, 10 percent in the United States, and 17 percent in China. Says Poignonnec, "My view is that retail will move online very quickly in Africa. E-commerce might reach 15 percent of total retail sales over the next ten years, and then it will go beyond that." He adds, "In the US, e-commerce is slowly changing centuries of old shopping habits. Here it is creating the habits. People are making their first big buys, like smartphones, and first online purchases simultaneously."[21]

Jumia, like Gro Intelligence, is proud of its record in helping other African entrepreneurs expand. It boasts a network of forty thousand active merchants across Africa, many of them small enterprises that are using e-commerce to reach new customers and grow their own businesses. Said Poignonnec:

"We are helping our merchants, whether they are e-commerce sellers or hotels or restaurants, go direct to the consumer and generate additional business. We're also helping them make big savings, as the cost to serve via the internet is much lower than in traditional retail. They also get valuable information: how many people have seen their product during the last twenty-four hours, what their conversion rate is, and what the impact is on sales if they change the price or launch a promotion." To help its merchants professionalize and build scale, Jumia runs training programs covering core business skills such as accounting and marketing.

In 2017, Jumia had over 2 million active customers in thirteen African countries. In that year, its sales reached nearly $600 million—and they had roughly doubled each year since 2013. Like many young, fast-growing e-commerce businesses worldwide, Jumia has not yet made a profit. That has not stopped investors pouring money into the business: it raised $326 million from Goldman Sachs, MTN, and others in 2016. Says Poignonnec: "We're comfortable about the fact that we're not yet profitable because we're on track with our plan, which is to really create scalable infrastructure for our e-commerce platform across Africa."

There is space for many other startups to build scale in Africa—whether in retail, technology, manufacturing, agriculture, mining, or a host of other sectors. The fact that Africa has fewer large firms than it should is indicative of a business arena that's wide open for entrepreneurs. You'll find no shortage of unmet demand. If you're a big thinker and a risk taker, and if your business plan is compelling enough, you'll find a legion of investors and supporters ready to help you grow.

One such backer is Tony Elumelu, founder of United Bank for Africa, a pan-African financial institution, and the Tony Elumelu Foundation. He has made it his mission to "create and empower more entrepreneurs" as a way to "democratize job creation." As he told us, "Only entrepreneurs can create the millions of jobs we need to power Africa's economies out of poverty. A vibrant, African-led private sector with significant participation from entrepreneurs is the key to unlocking Africa's economic and social potential." Elumelu has put his money where his mouth is: his foundation was committed to spending $100 million over ten years to identify, train, and fund ten thousand African entrepreneurs. His goal is that these entrepreneurs between them realize $10 billion in revenue and create 1 million jobs.

EXTRAORDINARY GROWTH AND PROFITABILITY BECKON—IF YOU HAVE THE RIGHT STRATEGY

Despite the huge opportunities we've just described, not every company will succeed in translating this potential into growth that is rapid, consistent, and profitable. In a marketplace that is both complex and increasingly competitive, there are huge differences in performance between the most successful companies and the rest. Some companies are the lions of African business, standing head and shoulders above the rest. Others risk becoming the lions' prey.

Consider the case of Tiger Brands, a major South Africa-based food company. In 2012 it paid Aliko Dangote nearly $200 million for a controlling stake in Dangote Flour Mills in Nigeria. But Tiger soon discovered that the Nigerian market was much more competitive than it had expected. Its troubles multiplied when the sudden drop in oil prices in 2014 sent Nigeria's economy and currency into a tailspin. Losses mounted, and Tiger ended up pouring another $180 million into the business before giving up and selling its stake back to Dangote in 2015—for one dollar.[22] (Dangote Flour Mills has since returned to profitability.)

In the banking sector, despite rapid overall growth, there have also been clear winners and losers. Between 2012 and 2017, banking revenues across the African continent grew nearly twice as fast as the global average, and Africa's banks were, on average, more than twice as profitable as those in developed markets in 2017. But the best-performing banks have benefited disproportionately from this buoyant market.[23] We analyzed the performance of thirty-five of Africa's largest banks from 2011 to 2016, and found that the top quintile grew their revenues at 23 percent a year over this period, more than double that of the bottom quintile. The banking lions were highly profitable, delivering an average return on equity (ROE) of 37 percent— quadruple that of their low-performing peers. The lions were also impressively lean: their average cost-to-income ratio over this period was 40 percent, compared with 57 percent for their slower-moving competitors. Their average credit loss ratio was exactly half that of the low performers.

The lions of African banking—including Kenya's Equity Bank and Commercial Bank of Africa, Nigeria's Guaranty Trust Bank (GTB), and South Africa's FirstRand Bank—have staked out an exciting future in the continent. But the market's high degree of competitiveness, combined with economic and political volatility, has challenged some other big banks. Their missteps have included investing in the wrong markets at the wrong time, paying insufficient attention to risk, and lagging their competitors in innovation.

HOW TO WIN IN AFRICA: A STRATEGIC GUIDE

Whichever sector you operate in, as is clear from the above example of the banking sector, not every company in Africa is benefiting equally from the continent's overall growth. That's why, in this book, we are so obsessed with the question: *What does it take to win in Africa?* We focus on pinpointing the strategic choices and operational steps that companies need to make if they are to translate the abundant opportunities of Africa into winning businesses. To create this strategic guide, we draw on McKinsey's global research on corporate strategy—but we animate it with the unique circumstances of Africa and the real-world experience of some of the continent's most successful companies.

Over a two-year period between 2014 and 2016, our colleagues in McKinsey's Strategy Practice analyzed three thousand of the world's largest companies to understand which achieved outsize profitability over time, which underperformed, and what accounted for the difference. The metric used in the analysis was *economic profit*, or economic value added—the profit a company generates after paying back its investors for the use of their capital.

The findings of this exercise were startling: the top 20 percent of companies make 90 percent of the world's economic profit. The 60 percent in the middle barely meet their cost of capital, and thus make no economic profit. And the bottom 20 percent generate negative economic profit, costing their investors an average of around $1 billion a year.[24]

Of course, profit is not the only metric that matters. As the success stories of many of Africa's lions demonstrate, a burning commitment to improving people's lives is often a major driver of corporate success—this is truly a continent where companies can do well by doing good. Yet few companies will consider themselves successful in the long run without meaningful shareholder returns. Healthy profits are also the fuel to power investment and growth, to support innovation, and to attract and nurture talented people.

So, what does it take to beat the odds and become one of the select few companies that turn market opportunities into enduring value? For one thing, McKinsey's research shows that picking the right geographic and industry trends is a key factor. Companies with exposure to high-growth cities, countries, and regions improve their odds. Likewise, companies that ride strong industry trends, such as rapid adoption of mobile and digital technology, have much better odds of outperforming. Sometimes those are "trends with a twist," such as Africa's large unserved markets or infrastructure gaps: to benefit from such trends, companies need the imagination to see unmet demand or unsolved problems as opportunities.

Just as important, outperformers make smart use of strategic moves—the steps that a company takes to shift its portfolio toward geographic and industry trends, or to double down on profitable growth if it is riding on strong tailwinds. These moves include frequent use of M&A and divestment; aggressively moving resources to the best opportunities; making significant capital investment; driving breakthrough productivity; and innovating the business model to improve the company's differentiation from competitors.

Last but not least, companies need the resources to invest in promising trends and execute bold strategic moves. Companies with sufficient funds for expansion outperform their peers—as do those that invest heavily in research and development.

We believe these elements provide a useful checklist for any company hoping to build a large-scale, high-performing business in Africa. Let's take another look at the example of SABMiller. It was early to spot the trends of Africa's rapid economic and population growth, as well as the continent's increasingly aspirational consumers, who were ready to switch from home brews to bottled lager. Then the company really proved its mettle when it came to strategic moves. It became an expert at M&A, even in challenging circumstances. It achieved industry-leading productivity. And it used its marketing savvy to create brands that won intense loyalty from African customers. All that was backed with real investment. Once SABMiller's leadership made African growth a priority, the brewer's local teams knew they would have the financial backing to grab acquisition opportunities when they came along and later build a string of new breweries.

We can't influence your company's degree of financial endowment, but we can encourage you to make your investments in Africa sizeable enough to achieve meaningful scale and impact, just as management teams and boards of companies like SABMiller, GE, Total, Jumia, and Ethiopian Airlines have done. When it comes to trends, we have plenty to say in chapter 2. You'll see that Africa has both geographic and industry trends in its favor, which is why it is such a promising long-term bet for companies in many sectors. But you'll also see that those trends come with a twist: unlocking Africa's growth potential requires imaginative problem-solving on issues ranging from infrastructure gaps to macroeconomic volatility.

In part 2, we turn to the strategic moves that your company will need to make if it is to win in Africa (see figure 1-5). These include a smart approach to geographic expansion, innovating your business model to increase your differentiation from competitors, and operational solutions that will help you manage risk and boost your company's resilience to

FIGURE 1-5

How to win in Africa

Map your Africa strategy

4 navigation tools:

- Set a clear aspiration for growth

- Prioritize the markets that matter most

- Define how you'll achieve scale and relevance

- Build the ecosystem you need to thrive

Innovate your business model

4 innovation practices:

- Create products and services that fulfill Africa's unmet needs

- Rethink your business model to truly engage with customers

- Get lean to drive down cost and price points

- Harness technology to unleash the next wave of innovation

Do well by doing good

Solve Africa's unmet needs to drive profitable, sustainable growth

Unleash Africa's talent

3 talent imperatives:

- Build vocational skills for frontline workers

- Create robust processes to grow talent from within

- Harness the power of inclusion—particularly women's advancement

Build resilience for the long term

4 cornerstones:

- Take a long-term view—and ride out short-term volatility

- Diversify to build a balanced portfolio

- Integrate up and down your value chain

- Understand local context and engage with governments

Africa's inevitable shocks. Last but not least, we highlight the approaches you can take to unleash Africa's talent, including nurturing vocational and managerial skills at scale and fostering a new kind of business leader for the African century ahead.

It's good news that Africa offers companies so much room to grow, because corporate growth has tremendous positive impact. Some years ago, a group of our McKinsey colleagues wrote a book called *The Alchemy of Growth*. Growth, they wrote, is "a noble pursuit. It creates new jobs for the community and wealth for shareholders. It can turn ordinary companies into stimulating environments where employees find a sense of purpose in their work."[25] Subsequent McKinsey research has confirmed that high-growth companies outperform their peers in their stock market valuation and are much better placed to fund new investments, attract great talent, and acquire assets.[26]

Wherever your company is headquartered, Africa offers you exciting opportunities for long-term growth. Yes, there will be challenges and pitfalls along the way, making it critical that you craft the right strategy and manage risks smartly. But we are convinced that the continent should be home to many more large, successful companies earning healthy returns for their shareholders and making a difference in millions of people's lives. Will your company be one of them?

CHAPTER 2

THE BIG FIVE

GROWTH TRENDS WITH A TWIST

By now, we hope we've convinced you that Africa is a key market to watch. But we've also made it clear that the lions of African business are outpacing their slower rivals, and sometimes eating them for lunch. The companies that turn Africa's opportunity into successful enterprises have a common starting point: their insight into the long-term growth trends under way across the continent.

Consider the example of digital payments. By some estimates, cash is used for more than 99 percent of payments in African countries such as Ethiopia and Nigeria; by contrast, digital channels account for more than half of all transactions in many European countries.[1] Cautious investors might see that gap as a barrier to growth—when economies are heavily cash-based, that hampers commerce, financial-services penetration, and credit issuance. But bolder thinkers see the transformative growth opportunity waiting to be unlocked. One such trend-spotter is

Mitchell Elegbe, a Nigerian engineer and entrepreneur. In 2002, he founded a company called Interswitch, with the mission to "connect Nigeria to the digital world." It has grown rapidly to become one of Africa's leading digital-payments providers: in 2017 it processed $38 billion in transaction value.

Today, Nigerian consumers and businesses make more than 300 million digital transactions a month across a suite of Interswitch-enabled channels. Backed by two leading private equity firms, UK-based Helios and US-based TA Associates, Interswitch plans to list on the London and Lagos stock exchanges in 2019. It could raise as much as $1 billion in its initial public offering.[2]

Elegbe told us how, back in 2002, he had observed his fellow Nigerians carrying piles of cash with them to pay for everything from groceries to cell phone airtime to utility bills. Debit and credit cards were a rarity, as were point-of-sale (POS) machines. ATMs, too, were few and far between, and each could be used only by customers of one bank, as Nigeria lacked the infrastructure for interbank ATM connectivity. The result was that people spent hours in banks queuing for cash, or simply kept it under the mattress to avoid the hassle.

Elegbe spotted a big unmet need and started Interswitch in order to address it. In its early years, the company built the first interbank transaction switching and payment processing infrastructure in Nigeria, which enabled interbank ATM sharing as well as the first real-time POS system. Its Paydirect platform revolutionized revenue collection for governments and large companies, while its online payment gateway, Webpay, opened the way for e-commerce in Nigeria. In 2008 it launched Verve, today Nigeria's most widely used card brand. The next year it introduced Quickteller, an online payment platform that is accessible via a wide variety of digital and physical channels;

today the platform has more than 15 million users. A more recent innovation is Paycode, which enables cardless transactions such as ATM withdrawals and POS payments, using a digital token. Interswitch is also helping unleash contactless payments in Africa: it is upgrading its systems to allow consumers to scan "quick response" barcodes from their cell phones.

In Elegbe's words, Interswitch's role is to "facilitate forms of exchange that are secure, convenient and consistent." Yet Elegbe sees many more opportunities to find digital solutions to Africans' daily challenges and grow his business. In 2017 Interswitch unveiled a bold five-year strategy to broaden its service offering both to businesses and to consumers and to expand its footprint in African countries beyond Nigeria. One key thrust of that strategy is to build up Interswitch's "financial inclusion" business, which helps banks, merchants, and mobile networks deliver digital-payment services to Africans who do not have bank accounts. There is plenty of room for that particular business to grow: in Nigeria alone, an estimated 55 million adults, more than half the total, fall into that category.[3]

Interswitch has identified a growth trend hidden in Africa's underdevelopment. As the continent's populations grow in size and spending power and large and small businesses multiply and expand, demand for digital solutions and infrastructure is exploding. Some basic solutions, like ATMs and POS machines, are widespread in the West but relatively scarce in Africa. Others, like Quickteller, are new solutions or adaptations that need to be "made in Africa." As Elegbe told us: "If the problem has already been solved, your business won't achieve sustainable growth. We sought out an opportunity with long-term growth potential, and then worked assiduously to realize that opportunity by providing people and businesses with full control over their finances."

As our global executive survey shows, businesses around the world are keenly aware of the opportunity presented by Africa's megatrends (see figure 2-1). But you need to parse those trends carefully, like Elegbe did, if you are to spot solvable problems with long-term growth potential. Our survey suggests that executives with on-the-ground experience often do a better job of identifying those opportunities. We asked respondents how many African nations they had visited for business or personal reasons. Among those who had visited multiple countries, more than three-quarters expected rapid economic growth in Africa over the coming decades. But only half of those who had never been to Africa thought the same.

Do local business executives see something that their global peers are missing? To help you find out, we'd like to invite you back onto the Land Rover to take a tour of what we call Africa's *big five*: powerful long-term growth trends that are awesome to behold, but that can be just as elusive and unpredictable as any beast in the wild. Here are those five big trends—and their twists:

1. A fast-growing, rapidly urbanizing population with rising spending power—but with average incomes still low by Western standards and high levels of economic inequality

2. A trillion-dollar opportunity to industrialize Africa, both to meet rising domestic demand and to create a bridge-head in global export markets—provided manufacturers can overcome a myriad of barriers ranging from power outages to trade barriers to productivity challenges

3. A big push by governments and the private sector to close Africa's infrastructure gaps, including those in electricity, transport, and water—although it will be a huge challenge to resolve the massive backlog

FIGURE 2-1

Megatrends create big opportunities for business

In our Africa business survey, digitization, consumer, and infrastructure stand out.

What trends and/or forces do you expect to be the biggest growth opportunities in Africa over the next 20 years?* % of respondents, n = 792

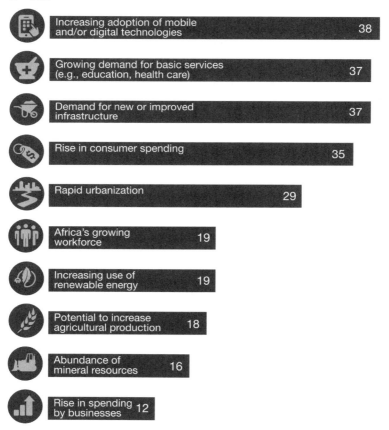

Increasing adoption of mobile and/or digital technologies — 38

Growing demand for basic services (e.g., education, health care) — 37

Demand for new or improved infrastructure — 37

Rise in consumer spending — 35

Rapid urbanization — 29

Africa's growing workforce — 19

Increasing use of renewable energy — 19

Potential to increase agricultural production — 18

Abundance of mineral resources — 16

Rise in spending by businesses — 12

*Respondents who answered "other" or "don't know/not applicable" are not shown. Question was asked only of respondents who said they have been to at least one country in Africa, for either personal or business reasons, and who said 5 percent or more of their organizations' current revenue is earned in Africa.

Source: McKinsey Insights executive survey on business in Africa, 2017.

4. Continued resource abundance in agriculture, mining, and oil and gas, with the prospect of rising innovation and investment in these sectors unlocking new food production, energy, and wealth for Africa—but, just like manufacturers, companies in these sectors must overcome steep barriers to realize that potential

5. Rapid adoption of mobile and digital technologies that could leapfrog Africa past many obstacles to growth— provided companies can marshal the investment funding and technical talent needed to overcome historic underdevelopment and achieve scale

TREND 1: A FAST-GROWING, URBANIZING POPULATION WITH BIG UNMET NEEDS

We believe that rising demand from African consumers and enterprises is one of the world's largest but least understood business opportunities. One factor driving that demand is sheer numbers. The continent will account for one-fifth of humanity by 2025, and will see its population double by the middle of this century. That will make it one of the only regions on earth with an expanding labor force and expanding group of consumers.

Already, between 2010 and 2015, Africa's working-age population increased by fourteen percentage points compared with nine percentage points in India and only one percentage point in China. In 2034, the continent is expected to have a larger working-age population than China or India, at 1.1 billion people. Africa's growing labor force makes the continent unusual in a broadly aging world. An expanding working-age population is associated with strong rates of GDP growth and offers a potential demographic dividend.[4] As Donald Kaberuka, past president of the African Development Bank (AfDB), told us: "The businesses that look properly at these long-term mega-trends will be the winners. And the most important of those long-term trends are around demographics. Whether you're providing health care, housing, education, or infrastructure for growing cities, that is where the business opportunities will lie."

Indeed, Africa is in the midst of an historic shift from a rural, agriculture-based economy to a diversified urban economy. More than 80 percent of its population growth over the next few decades will occur in cities, making it the fastest-urbanizing region in the world. By 2030, Africa will have seventeen cities with more than 5 million inhabitants each—up from only six in 2015. Some, like Addis Ababa and Nairobi, will be familiar names to global companies. Others, like Ibadan and Kano in Nigeria, and Ouagadougou in Burkina Faso, are less likely to be on corporate radar screens. Western investors will have an even harder time identifying the dozens of midsize cities across the continent: by 2030, there will be eighty-nine African cities with populations of 1 million or more (figure 2-2).[5]

Knowing your way around Africa's fast-growing cities is critical if your business is to participate in the continent's growth. Throughout history, income has risen in tandem with urbanization and industrialization. That was true in eighteenth-century England and Europe, nineteenth-century America, and twentieth-century Japan, and it's true now in China, India, Africa, and other emerging markets. People are leaving their farms behind, getting more productive jobs, and learning new skills in cities—and raising their income by a factor of two or more. As they do so, they provide the consumption, labor, and entrepreneurial spirit to support the emergence of an increasingly sophisticated and profitable business sector.

FIGURE 2-2

Africa's cities are growing rapidly

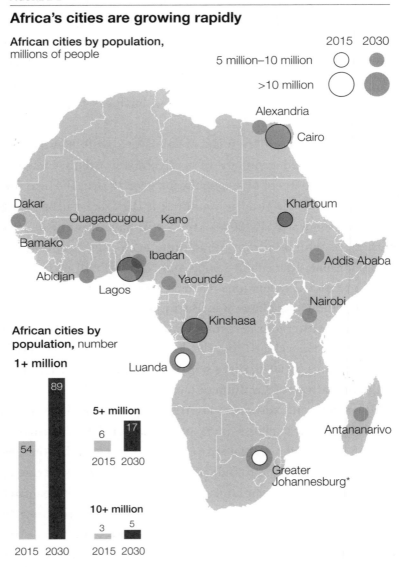

African cities by population,
millions of people

2015 2030

5 million–10 million

>10 million

Alexandria
Cairo
Dakar
Khartoum
Ouagadougou Kano
Bamako
Ibadan
Addis Ababa
Abidjan
Lagos
Yaoundé
Nairobi
Kinshasa

African cities by
population, number

1+ million

89

54

2015 2030

Luanda

5+ million

6 17

2015 2030

10+ million

3 5

2015 2030 2015 2030

Antananarivo

Greater
Johannesburg*

*Greater Johannesburg includes the City of Johannesburg, Ekurhuleni, and the West Rand.

Source: United Nations World Population Prospect, June 2014 revision, UN population
division; MGI Cityscope; McKinsey Global Institute analysis.

The difference is that today this process happens much more quickly. In 1975, only 25 percent of Africans lived in cities; by 2015, that share had risen to 40 percent. Around 2037, Africa will have shifted to a majority-urban population.[6]

Paul Collier, professor of economics and public policy at Oxford University's Blavatnik School of Government, is one of the foremost experts on urbanization in Africa and the developing world.[7] As he pointed out to us, "Between now and 2050, Africa's urban population will triple—so two-thirds of Africa's urban space has yet to be built. That's the vital struggle: to get the coming two-thirds better than the existing third." Collier worries that Africa's urbanization is producing "congested sprawl," and that, without better connectivity and clearer land rights, the continent risks losing out on the productivity gains that other urbanizing regions have achieved. But he points to a few fast-growing African cities, including Addis Ababa in Ethiopia and Kigali in Rwanda, that are investing ahead of the curve in infrastructure, and showing the way to others.

Collier is also cautiously optimistic about Lagos. With as many as 21 million people, Nigeria's commercial capital is Africa's largest city and is often seen as an urban-planning nightmare. "If you visit Lagos for the first time, the chances are you'll be horrified," he said. "But if you've been going there for forty years, as I have, it's a remarkable improvement on what it was." Collier credits three successive, democratically elected governors of Lagos state. Over a period of eighteen years, they have boosted the city's tax base, built much-needed roads and bridges, and brought greater order to the metropolis after its neglect under military rule in the 1980s and 1990s. As Collier put it, the task facing Lagos's government is to "retrofit from disaster." It's a huge challenge, but, he notes, "certainly the government of the moment understands the problem. In many respects, Lagos is Africa's most important city of the future. If Lagos can be got right, that's a huge success for the continent."

Akinwunmi Ambode, the governor of Lagos State, told us about his bold plans to make Lagos a better city. His vision is to double the city region's GDP, and he is pushing major infrastructure, educational, and health-care advances—including installing streetlights on a large scale, building a rail- and waterway-based mass transit network, expanding vocational training, and developing new public health facilities. He is also finding imaginative ways to close Lagos's multibillion-dollar infrastructure gap, including use of public–private partnerships.

A $4 TRILLION MARKET—BUT CAN YOU SERVE IT PROFITABLY?

Africa's fast-growing, urbanizing population already represents a sizeable market—and it's only getting more attractive. We estimate that private consumption in Africa rose from $860 billion in 2008 to $1.4 trillion in 2015—significantly higher than that of India, which has a similar population size. We forecast that it could reach $2.1 trillion by 2025.[8] The business-to-business market represents an even larger opportunity. In 2015, companies in Africa spent some $2.6 trillion building factories, buying equipment and services, and gearing up to serve customers across the continent. We expect annual spending by African businesses to reach $3.5 trillion by 2025.

Which companies are best positioned to benefit from this trend? African consumers surveyed by McKinsey say that clothes, appliances, and gadgets are the top items they plan to purchase next.[9] There is also rapid growth in spending on discretionary categories such as soft drinks, alcoholic beverages, and meat.

Zambeef, a Zambia-based food company that does everything from raising cattle, hogs, and poultry to manning supermarket meat departments, has ridden this wave to great effect. Zambeef has grown from a staff of sixty in 1994 to over seven thousand today, selling steaks and chops to higher-income supermarket shoppers in sub-Saharan Africa and beef liver, chicken feet, and other inexpensive cuts to small shops catering to lower-income customers. Since there is no cold-chain logistics in Zambia, or indeed most of Africa, Zambeef runs its own fleet of refrigerated delivery trucks. It controls the entire value chain, even producing its own animal feed. After its livestock are slaughtered for market, a Zambeef subsidiary tans the hides, turning some of them into shoes. The company's revenues climbed from $160 million in 2010 to $220 million in 2016.[10]

Just as organizations like Zambeef have experienced rapid growth, however, some international consumer goods firms have struggled to achieve profitability in Africa. In 2015, for example, Swiss-based foods company Nestlé announced it was scaling back its African business. One of its executives was quoted as saying: "We thought this would be the next Asia, but we have realized the middle class in the region is extremely small . . . urbanization is usually very good for manufacturers, but in this case many people are literally living in slums, so they have nothing to spend."[11]

What's the true picture? We find that more than 50 million African households—around 30 percent of the total—already have incomes above $5,000 a year. This may sound low by Western standards, but it's the level at which people typically begin spending more than half their income on discretionary items. We expect that number to exceed 70 million households by 2025. The number of "global consumer" households—those earning $20,000 or more—is also growing, and is likely to top 10 million by 2025. Of course, a dollar in Africa stretches much further than it does in the West. If we apply purchasing power parity (PPP) to Africa's consumer numbers, the opportunity looks even more favorable. By this measure, more than 70 percent of African households will have discretionary income by 2025, and more than a quarter will be global consumers. Affluent consumers, mostly concentrated in the North African countries and South Africa, are also on the rise.

AFRICA'S DISPARITIES, AND HOW TO NAVIGATE THEM

Hidden in all these numbers are extreme disparities in income and wealth. Kenya's capital, Nairobi, clearly shows those extremes. On the one hand, there's Karen, a serene neighborhood ten miles from downtown, where stately homes tucked inside lush gardens sell for upward of $1 million. But Nairobi is also home to Kibera, the largest slum in Africa, whose seven hundred thousand inhabitants have little electricity, limited water, and only crude sanitation facilities. Kibera is often the first stop for Kenyans moving to the city from remote rural villages.

These two neighborhoods are a reminder of Africa's high degree of income inequality. Companies seeking to tap the African consumer opportunity must understand the residents of Karen and Kibera alike and make explicit choices about which slice of the market to serve, with which products and services, at what price points. They must also be ready to compete with the informal vendors who command some 70 percent of Kenya's consumer spending. Take a walk round Nairobi's bustling streets and you'll see those entrepreneurs in all their variety. One sidewalk might serve as an informal shoe store, with a dozen merchants ready to haggle with bargain-hunting passersby. Another might be a food market selling freshly prepared meals for less than a dollar, from *ugali* (cornmeal) to spicy beef stew. Fittingly for a place whose nickname is "the green city in the sun," some of Nairobi's roadsides are home to bountiful informal nurseries selling a dazzling array of flowering plants.

That said, there is clearly a place for modern commerce in cities like Nairobi—and not just to serve consumers who live in places like Karen. The city is home to dozens of shopping malls built both by local developers and by international investors from South Africa, China, and elsewhere. Global supermarket chain Carrefour opened three major stores in 2016 and 2017, Botswana-based Choppies has also built a presence in Nairobi, and South Africa–based Shoprite announced in 2017 that it too was entering the Kenyan market. Meanwhile, e-commerce sites such as Jumia and Kilimall are doing brisk business, selling everything from tee shirts to toasters, while the city's "Silicon Savannah" tech ecosystem is spawning startups like MyDawa ("my medicine" in Swahili), which delivers prescription drugs and other wellness products to 150 secure pickup points across Nairobi.

Companies seeking to serve African consumers must also take into account the fact that the continent's households—like their societies—are in a state of transition. Many emerging or middle-income consumers must support family members, or save or invest to guard against economic volatility. For example, a thirty-three-year-old Kenyan who works in a bank earns enough to buy appliances such as a fridge and a television. But he is also helping pay for his younger siblings' education, and he has invested in a small farm. Companies that help such young Africans to save and invest for the future, rather than just seeing them as consumers, are more likely to build sustainable businesses.

The key is to take a longer-term view on Africa's consumers. To gauge who those will be and what they will buy, it's worth reviewing the experience of other emerging markets. One of us (Georges) moved to China in 1999 and spent seven years helping global and local companies understand and serve that country's rapidly rising consumer market. As Chinese consumers urbanized and earned steadily higher incomes, the products they bought followed a distinct development curve—one that brought new opportunities for companies in many different sectors. Initially, consumers' spending was concentrated on food and essentials such as bicycles. As their incomes rose, they increased their spending on furniture, and then on televisions, mobile phones, appliances, and fashion. Finally, as they entered the affluent bracket, they began purchasing cars, apartments, and houses as well as services such as private health care.

That provides a useful lesson for companies in Africa: focus not just on what consumers are buying today, but on what they will be looking at five or ten years from now.

TREND 2: AFRICA'S COMING
INDUSTRIAL REVOLUTION

Hawassa, 170 miles south of Addis Ababa in the Great Rift Valley of central Ethiopia, is a modestly popular tourist town with a population of 350,000. Local and even foreign visitors come to stroll the cobblestone paths along Lake Awassa, the smallest of the Great Rift lakes, which boasts its own pod of hippopotamus. Tourists can rent bikes for the picturesque twenty-eight-mile ride around the lake.

Lately, however, Hawassa has been host to another kind of visitor. Three miles from the lakefront sprawls the Hawassa Industrial Park. Phase 1, which opened in 2017, is a grid of thirty-seven giant red and gray metal sheds covering two hundred and forty-seven acres.[12] Inside, workers at airy workstations churn out shirts, jackets, and socks for labels such as Tommy Hilfiger and Calvin Klein—as well as garment companies from China, Hong Kong, and India—at machines that run mostly on renewable hydroelectric power. They are part of a wave of investment that is making Ethiopia a significant manufacturing exporter: its apparel exports increased nearly sevenfold between 2010 and 2015.

Hawassa is the showcase project of the Ethiopian government's vision of establishing "dirt-to-shirt" textile hubs. Rather than trying to retrofit a modern industrial plant onto aging legacy infrastructure, this industrial park started with a greenfield location, carefully chosen and ambitiously developed. Hawassa is close to the country's cotton fields in the Awash Valley. Visitors from Addis Ababa can reach the park in under an hour via a forty-minute flight into its new airport. A highway linking Hawassa with the capital is nearing completion, and a rail line to the Port of Djibouti is being extended to speed finished goods to the export market. Even the local university is expanding to better train workers for the new industry.

Over the past decade, some manufacturing sectors have become internationally competitive and achieved rapid growth. In addition to Ethiopia's apparel exports, the automotive sectors in Morocco and South Africa increased exports and Egypt increased exports of chemicals and electrical machinery. These examples suggest that some African countries have the opportunity to grow competitive manufacturing exports on a much larger scale than is the case today—and to take on production from "Factory China" as that country's labor costs rise.[13] In addition, Africa currently imports much of what it consumes, representing an even bigger opportunity to expand local industry, particularly given the fast-growing demand from local consumer and B2B markets.

In our *Lions on the Move* research, we calculated that Africa has an opportunity to double its manufacturing output to nearly $1 trillion by 2025.[14] We see major opportunities to meet growing local demand for "global innovation" products such as automobiles and chemicals, as well as for processed goods such as food and beverages, and resource-intensive manufacturing such as cement and petroleum (figure 2-3). Indeed, three-quarters of the growth opportunity in manufacturing lies in meeting intra-African demand and substituting imports. The remaining one-quarter would come from accelerating growth in niche manufacturing exports.

A doubling of Africa's manufacturing output would be a win for both business and societies. We estimate it would result in the creation of 6 million to 14 million stable jobs directly in the manufacturing sector by 2025, increasing the number of stable jobs in Africa by as much as 11 percent.[15]

FIGURE 2-3

Africa could double its manufacturing output in a decade

Potential revenue growth from African manufacturers by 2025

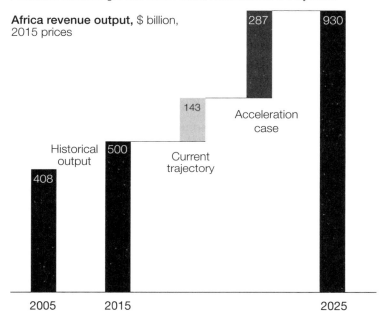

Africa revenue output, $ billion, 2015 prices

Historical output

Current trajectory

Acceleration case

287 | 930
408 | 500 | 143

2005 2015 2025

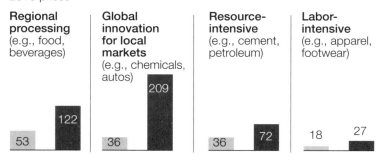

Current trajectory versus acceleration case, by key sector, $ billion, 2015 prices

Regional processing (e.g., food, beverages)	Global innovation for local markets (e.g., chemicals, autos)	Resource-intensive (e.g., cement, petroleum)	Labor-intensive (e.g., apparel, footwear)
53 / 122	36 / 209	36 / 72	18 / 27

Source: IHS; UNCTAD; McKinsey Global Institute analysis.

HOW AFRICAN MANUFACTURERS
CAN SUBSTITUTE IMPORTS

As brewers and beverage companies have ramped up production across Africa, they have had to import much of their packaging. That created an opportunity for GZ Industries (GZI) to build Nigeria's first aluminum-can manufacturing plant in 2010, in Ogun State near Lagos. GZI, founded by a group of private investors and subsequently backed by several local and international private equity firms, sank millions into the 430,000-square-mile plant—which boasts state-of-the-art equipment imported from Europe and the United States.

Danladi Verheijen, managing director of Verod Capital Management, GZI's early backer, told us: "We saw a massive opportunity. It just made no sense to import aluminum cans from across the ocean. There was significant existing demand, supply chains were already developed, and the benefits were obvious for our customers like Nigerian Breweries (owned by Heineken), Guinness, and Coca-Cola." GZI's first plant quickly reached its production capacity of 1.2 billion cans a year, leading the company to open a second plant in Abia State in southeastern Nigeria in 2014. GZI plans to expand across Africa, including establishing a plant in South Africa, where it will go head-to-head with Nampak, currently the largest can manufacturer in Africa.[16]

Of course, manufacturing even a relatively simple product such as aluminium cans is often a challenging undertaking; barriers ranging from power shortages to bureaucratic impediments to skills gaps drive up costs and risk. Yet, as many manufacturers have demonstrated, those that can adapt their business models to cope with these barriers can find wide-open opportunities. In fact, many of today's successful African manufacturers—including the Dangote Group—started life as importers, but later realized that with their intimate knowledge of the market, the savings achievable by cutting out shipping and tariff costs would more than justify their investment in local manufacturing plants. In many cases—like that of Ethiopia's Hawassa hub—industrial policies put in place by African governments have created incentives that have supported those investments.

The experience of Chinese-owned manufacturing firms in Africa shines a spotlight on the opportunity of import substitution. A McKinsey research project found that Chinese companies already handle an estimated 12 percent of Africa's industrial production. This share suggests a replication of some of China's manufacturing might in Africa, with Chinese manufacturing executives increasingly drawn to Africa's relatively high margins for a range of manufactured goods.

Many of the Chinese manufacturers we interviewed said they were hoping to replicate their success in China, where their factories employed widely available low-cost labor. In Africa, they are moving faster, as they have found ready local markets where they can substitute expensive imports with their own products. Indeed, unlike in China, Chinese factories in Africa are largely serving domestic markets; 93 percent of the revenues of manufacturers we spoke to came from local or regional sales. Among the firms we looked at, more than half reported that they had taken three years or less to make back their initial investment. For example, a manufacturer in Kenya said, "I expect to make back my investment in less than a year because the prevailing market price is so high for my product."[17]

We estimate that African manufacturers—both local and foreign—could more than double their sales to intra-African markets by 2025, increasing their annual revenue by

$326 billion.[18] Import substitution makes up a large proportion of that opportunity: Africa imports a large percentage of goods in many categories that could be produced more easily and more cheaply locally. For example, it imports one-third of the food, beverages, and other processed goods it consumes—and two-thirds of its supply of advanced manufacturing products such as cars and machinery.

FROM AFRICA TO THE WORLD: THE EXPORT OPPORTUNITY

Can Africa be a large-scale exporter of advanced manufacturing goods such as automobiles? If you have doubts, take a look at Morocco. The North African nation's automotive industry multiplied its export revenue by a factor of 12, from $0.4 billion in 2004 to $5 billion in 2015, an annual growth rate of 26 percent. The automotive sector alone added sixty-seven thousand jobs between 2004 and 2015. French automakers Renault and Peugeot have together invested more than $2 billion to create assembly capacity for 650,000 cars and 200,000 engines a year. Morocco has also attracted an ecosystem of global automotive suppliers including Delphi/Aptiv, Linamar, and Simoldes. It has also achieved notable export-led growth in other segments such as aerospace. Morocco has leveraged two distinct advantages: its proximity to large European markets and labor costs that are around one-third those of even the lowest-cost European countries. Morocco's government adopted a series of industrial acceleration plans to explicitly build on these advantages to power rapid industrialization.[19]

Morocco's success is one indicator of the opportunity to leverage Africa's relatively low costs and its proximity to major markets to build successful export businesses of both goods and services. Previous McKinsey research estimated that African firms could increase their export revenue by more than $100 billion by 2025.[20] Three-quarters of this would come from exports in advanced manufacturing products such as cars and chemicals. But there is also a real opportunity to increase exports of labor-intensive goods, such as apparel, and space to scale up both Africa's service exports and tourism offerings.[21] Labor-intensive products, in particular, offer an opportunity for countries with traditionally small manufacturing bases to industrialize their economies while also creating significant numbers of jobs. For example, Vietnam and Bangladesh added 3.7 million and 5.2 million manufacturing jobs, respectively, between 2000 and 2014, many of them related to labor-intensive exports.

Companies making labor-intensive goods in Africa have the opportunity to capitalize on the shift in manufacturing jobs away from China, whose advantage, based in part on low labor costs, is fast eroding: average Chinese hourly wages have risen from $0.43 in 2000 to $2.88 in 2013, an annual increase of 16 percent.[22] In many of Africa's low-income manufacturing nations, labor costs are closer to China's in 2000. Some countries have already translated this advantage into rapid growth in labor-intensive manufacturing exports. Tanzania, for instance, has achieved annual growth in such exports of 9 percent since 2004; Ethiopia's labor-intensive manufacturing exports have grown at 12 percent a year.[23]

As our colleague Irene Yuan Sun argues, these African countries are already providing proof of a theory in development economics called the *flying geese paradigm*, which posits that "manufacturing companies act like migrating geese, flying from country to country as costs and demand change."[24] According to this analogy, factories from a leading country are forced by labor-price pressures to invest in a follower country, helping it accumulate ownership and move up the technology curve. This movement shifts the bulk of economic activity in the follower country from low-productivity agriculture and informal services to high-productivity manufacturing. The follower country eventually becomes a leading country, spawning companies in search of new production locations. The paradigm offers a convincing model of how Asian economies developed—in a chain from Japan to the Asian Tigers to China. It also suggests that with the right policies and long-term vision, Africa could become the next global manufacturing hub, not just of clothing and processed food but also of cars, machinery, chemicals, and other advanced manufactures.

OVERCOMING OBSTACLES TO MANUFACTURING GROWTH

Brooks Washington, founder of investment company Roha, is so confident of Africa's potential for industrialization that he has made the development of manufacturing plants a core focus of his business. Yet Washington is quick to emphasize the risks involved, including getting access to suitable land and sufficient capital, complying with local regulations, and ensuring sufficient power supply. Indeed, his firm exists to help local and global partners and investors manage and mitigate such risks. His advice to manufacturers looking to expand in Africa is: "Have a vision and a plan for the long term. There will be tough times; what's important is that you survive them and stay focused on the long-term prize."

Vera Songwe, executive secretary of the United Nations Economic Commission for Africa, is also concerned about the barriers to industrialization and economic diversification, and she is committed to helping solve them. "We're seeing more and more companies coming in to Africa and wanting to set up manufacturing industries," she told us. "But many struggle to get land: it takes a long time to get the necessary permits, especially if you're trying to find land to build new facilities. Some companies spend six months trying to understand which agency is responsible for releasing land for industry. I think this is going to be the big bottleneck: if you're coming in to set up productive capacities, you need space—most often in semi-urban areas." Songwe also sees access to reliable, competitive, stable electricity supply as a "big, big constraint" to industrialization. To unlock Africa's industrialization opportunity and build successful manufacturing businesses, companies will often need to work together with governments and local development agencies to put these basics for manufacturing in place.

Manufacturing hubs such as Hawassa are one effective solution. Songwe emphasizes that such hubs are not a substitute for comprehensive, business-enabling reforms by African countries—but she believes that "industrial zones and specialized regions are very important in some cases." One advantage is that they make it possible for private energy providers to invest in large-scale electrification. She told us, "An energy investor can come in and say, 'I will provide energy for seven or eight companies.'" That, in turn, frees manufacturers to focus on their core business.

Songwe points to another critical challenge for Africa's industrialists: skills. "In most industrial sectors, it's not easy to find a ready-to-go, skilled labor force," she said. She stresses that both private-sector firms and national governments must "make a big commitment to training and upgrading labor to meet the market's needs." Ideally, manufacturers should partner with governments to design and deliver targeted vocational training programs to build industry-relevant skills, as the auto manufacturers in Morocco have done. Within their businesses, many African manufacturers will need to embrace performance improvements and enhanced management training if they are to compete on a global stage.

TREND 3: AFRICA'S INFRASTRUCTURE GAP—AND THE BIG PUSH TO CLOSE IT

In 2017, Jack Ma, founder of Chinese e-commerce giant Alibaba, spoke to an audience of young entrepreneurs in Nairobi. Reflecting on his own experience in building a business in China, he said: "If the government does not have a solution to any problem, it is an opportunity. If people complain, it is an opportunity."[25] We recommend that businesses adopt that mindset when it comes to Africa's big infrastructure gaps.

The continent trails the BRIC countries (Brazil, Russia, India, and China) in key measures including electric power consumption per capita, rail density, and road density (figure 2-4). Dr. Akinwumi Adesina, president of the AfDB, puts electrification at the "very top of the list" of priorities for business development in Africa: "The major challenge that so many companies face in Africa is lack of electricity, which drives up the cost of doing business," he told us. Energy is like blood in the life of an economy—it is the key to getting businesses to work, whether you're in the banking sector, the agricultural sector, or mining sector, and whether you're a large company or a small or medium-size enterprise."

FIGURE 2-4

Most African countries lag other emerging markets in infrastructure

Electric power consumption, kilowatt hours per person

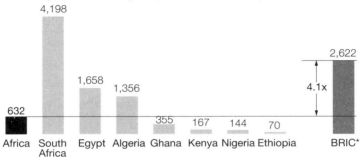

Rail density, kilometers of track per square km

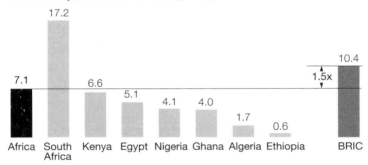

Road density, kilometers of road per square km

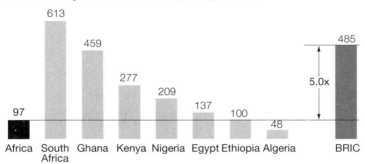

*Brazil, Russia, India, and China. Comparisons exclude Russia for roads and rail.

Source: World Bank, World Development Indicators Database; CIA, World Factbook.

The power gap is much more pronounced in some countries than in others. South Africa and the North African nations are relatively well supplied with electricity, but electricity consumption per person in Ethiopia, Kenya, and Nigeria is less than one-tenth that of the BRICs. In Mali, a typical household uses less electricity in a year than a Londoner uses to boil a kettle each day.[26] And nearly 600 million people in sub-Saharan Africa lack access to electricity altogether—with the result that whole communities literally live half their lives in the dark. The electric power gap imposes high costs on businesses too. Among the executives we surveyed, one-third said their companies generate their own electrical power or have backup generators on-site. Mobile phone provider MTN is one. In many of the countries it operates in, it runs a generator at every one of its base stations. Because by some measures, generator-based power costs three to six times what grid consumers pay across the world, it costs the company a reported $22 million a year in Nigeria alone.[27]

Companies doing business in Africa must face the electricity gap head on—not just generating their own power, but also finding ways to serve power-starved customers and to work with governments, development institutions, and other businesses to ramp up the continent's power supply. Harvard Business School professor Clayton Christensen neatly summarizes the outlook needed: "The recognition that 600 million people in Africa don't have access to electricity should be a spur to innovation, not a flag of caution."[28] If there is one company that embodies that can-do approach, it is M-Kopa. In just a few years, the Kenya-based startup has sold solar-power kits to hundreds of thousands of mostly rural households. (We explore its story in detail in part 2.)

More such initiatives are needed: McKinsey forecasts that Africa's demand for electricity will quadruple between 2010 and 2040. By then, sub-Saharan Africa alone will require as much electricity as India and Latin America combined did in 2010, and there is a big question mark about whether governments, utilities, and the private sector can manage the massive build-out of capacity needed to meet that demand.[29]

AFRICA'S RISING INFRASTRUCTURE SPEND

There is no shortage of effort to close Africa's infrastructure gaps. The continent's spending on infrastructure amounted to $80 billion in 2015—more than double the annual average in the first six years of this century. The rising spend has come from African governments, international development institutions, and private investors. Increasingly, it has come from China's state-linked institutions, which in 2015 contributed more than one-quarter of total infrastructure investment in Africa. Chinese infrastructure commitments grew at an average annual rate of 16 percent from 2012 to 2015 and have supported many of Africa's most ambitious infrastructure developments; Chinese contractors account for nearly half of Africa's international engineering, procurement, and construction (EPC) market.

Increased investment is already making a difference in people's daily lives. One example is the state-of-the-art Mombasa-Nairobi Standard Gauge Railway in Kenya, opened in 2017, cutting travel time between the cities in half. The Exim Bank of China financed more than 90 percent of the $3.6 billion project. Many more such projects are needed, however. As a share of GDP, infrastructure investment in Africa has remained at around 3.5 percent since 2000—but MGI estimates that this will need to rise to 4.5 percent if the continent is to close its infrastructure gap. In absolute terms, this means doubling annual investment in African infrastructure to $150 billion by 2025. Based on benchmark levels of spending, Africa's annual investment in power infrastructure will need to rise from $33 billion to around $55 billion in 2025, while annual investment in transport infrastructure will need to increase from $20 billion in 2015 to around $45 billion in 2025. Major additional investment will also be needed in water and telecoms infrastructure.[30]

A BIG ROLE FOR THE PRIVATE SECTOR

The private sector can play a critical role in delivering new infrastructure. Consider GE, which in recent years has ramped up its presence in the continent, established a regional headquarters in Nairobi, and signed "country-to-company" agreements with several African governments. Its agreement with Nigeria supports the financing, design, and building of vital infrastructure, including developing ten thousand megawatts of power-generation capacity, upgrading airports, modernizing and expanding the national railway corporation's locomotives, and constructing public hospitals and diagnostic centers. After Nigeria privatized some of its power generation assets, GE also worked with the new owners to ramp up power production.[31]

Jay Ireland, president and CEO of GE Africa, describes this approach as "an umbrella agreement matching our capabilities as a company with the issues the country was facing, including putting more power on the grid, strengthening logistics, and improving health-care outcomes." The agreements are "a two-way street, with accountability on both sides," Ireland told us.

While GE committed to deliver the outcomes in the agreement, those outcomes depended on Nigeria's long-term commitment to infrastructure development and its willingness to step in to solve bottlenecks. Besides supplying turbines and other equipment to help build the electrical grid in Africa, GE has also built a large-scale distributed power business, in which companies are able to generate their own power at the point of use.

Tidjane Thiam, CEO of Credit Suisse, believes such private-sector investments and innovations could be catalytic for infrastructure development in Africa. As a one-time chair of the G20 High Level Panel for Infrastructure Investment, he should know. He gives the example of toll bridges, which he helped pioneer as Minister of Planning and Development of Côte d'Ivoire in the 1990s. "At the time, people said there was no way it would work, but it often takes just one successful example to prove a concept," he told us. Today there are many privately financed toll bridges and toll roads in operation or construction across the continent. Companies investing in infrastructure in Africa must be ready to be "pioneers at the frontier of development," Thiam said; if those pioneers are smart about managing risk, they will reap rich rewards down the line. "In infrastructure development, most of the risk is in the early stages. Once you've built the asset, be it a power plant or a factory, the risk goes down by multiples." He added that targeted interventions by multilateral institutions can do much to mitigate the early-stage risk in infrastructure projects.

One such intervention, by the AfDB, is the creation of Africa50, an infrastructure investment platform focusing on high-impact national and regional projects in the energy, transport, information technology, and water sectors.[32] "Our goal is also to tap long-term savings from within and outside Africa by helping create an asset class attractive to institutional investors," said CEO Alain Ebobissé. "We are doing this by increasing the number of viable, bankable private and PPP projects . . . as well as by investing in later-stage private and PPP projects." The purpose, he said, is to "contribute to the development of Africa's infrastructure as quickly and broadly as possible."[33]

The AfDB is driving a broader campaign to "light up and power Africa" as the first in its "High 5" strategic priorities. It has committed $12 billion to energy projects between 2017 and 2022, and hopes to attract a further $45 billion to $50 billion in private sector investment.[34] The Power Africa program launched by US president Barack Obama in June 2013 has also enlisted the private sector in the electrification effort. As of 2017, it had leveraged more than $40 billion in commitments from the private sector to add nearly seven thousand megawatts in generating capacity across the continent.[35]

THE CHALLENGE OF SPRAWL: BUILDING BETTER AFRICAN CITIES

Beyond electricity, Africa faces other serious infrastructure gaps. For example, nearly a third of African households lack access to running water, and issues with reliable water supply are a challenge for many businesses too. And more than a fifth of respondents to our survey cited unreliable logistics and transportation infrastructure as one of the most serious barriers to operating a business in Africa. This affects their employees as well: while a few cities, such as Addis Ababa, have state-of-the-art rail and bus systems, transport networks in many of Africa's burgeoning cities are hugely inadequate to commuters' needs. Two of Africa's largest cities—Johannesburg and

Nairobi—have been included in a global index of the top five most painful cities for commuters.[36] Given our own experience in Lagos's traffic jams, we would add it to the list.

As mentioned earlier, urbanization expert Paul Collier believes that "congested sprawl" is one of the greatest risks to Africa's economic development. As he told us, "In a modern economy, you need three different types of connectivity to enable scale and specialization. You need firms to connect to workers. You need firms to connect to customers. And you need firms to connect to each other. That high degree of connectivity takes place in a well-functioning city." But many African cities, he warned, "are not urbanizing in a form that achieves connectivity." As a result, "individual firms just avoid the place altogether . . . or those firms become very dispersed around the city."

African cities need to design and deliver efficient mass transit systems to reduce the daily commute and increase business connectivity. McKinsey estimates that investing in better public transportation, alongside strategies to densify urban development, could give back more than one week a year to Africa's urban commuters.[37] To support healthy urbanization more broadly, Africa's urban managers also need to plan in a concerted way to avoid the pitfalls of unmanaged urbanization and ensure that urban growth translates into sustainable economic development. That includes encouraging densification rather than urban sprawl, especially informal urban sprawl.[38]

INFRASTRUCTURE FOR LEARNING AND HEALTH

Beyond core infrastructure, there are also many areas where companies are partnering with African governments to strengthen the provision of basic services. In Liberia, Bridge

International Academies is the main partner in a government pilot scheme that involves state-funded private operators running public primary schools. The government established the program in an effort to transform the performance of the country's school system: in 2013, none of Liberia's twenty-five thousand school-leavers passed the university entrance exam.

There are also opportunities for innovative partnerships in health care. In Kenya, GE secured a $230 million PPP contract to supply diagnostic equipment, such as ultrasound and electrocardiograph machines, to ninety-eight state hospitals, and to equip eleven intensive care units. The contract, signed in 2015, obliges GE to keep the machines in working order at least 95 percent of the time. GE employs a staff of nearly one hundred field engineers to deliver on this promise. The company reports that its health-care business makes good margins in Africa, and it considers its Kenyan model exportable to other countries.[39]

TREND 4: AFRICA'S UNTAPPED RESOURCE WEALTH—AND NEW INNOVATIONS TO UNLEASH IT

Africa has long been known for its resource abundance. It is blessed with vast tracts of arable land, and climatic conditions in many parts of the continent are highly conducive to agriculture. The continent's endowment of mineral resources— which are still underexplored and underexploited—is just as rich. To date, though, Africa has struggled to translate these resources into shared wealth and sustained economic developments. New innovations and investments promise to change that picture.

TURNING AFRICA INTO THE BREADBASKET OF THE WORLD: OPPORTUNITIES IN AGRICULTURE

The productivity of Africa's farming sector, which is dominated by smallholders, has long lagged that of other regions. Nigeria, for example, has as many as 30 million smallholders, producing more than 90 percent of the country's farm output. They are typically subsistence farmers who grow only enough for their own needs. As a result, although Nigeria has more than 80 million acres of arable land, it relies heavily on imported food. Its food import bill, according to the United Nations, is about $6 billion a year.

That has prompted a coalition of entrepreneurs, development institutions, and governments across the continent to work together to unlock a "green revolution" in Africa. Consider the example of Nigeria-based Babban Gona ("great farm" in Hausa), a social enterprise serving networks of smallholder farmers. Its members receive development and training, credit, agricultural inputs, marketing support, and other key services. Since its founding in 2010, Babban Gona has enlisted more than twenty thousand farmers, who have on average more than doubled their yields and increased their net income to 3.5 times that of the average farmer. Participating smallholder farmers, who are typically considered a high credit risk, have a 99.9 percent repayment rate on credit obtained via the program.[40]

Babban Gona's founder is a Nigerian-American, Kola Masha, managing director of impact investment company Doreo Partners. His goal is to enlist 1 million farmers in the program by 2025, providing livelihoods for 5 million people. That will not only boost Nigeria's food production, but will also help tackle the challenge of youth unemployment in a country with a large and fast-growing population. Says Masha: "We urgently need to create as many jobs as the entire population of Germany."[41]

Smallholder-focused programs like Babban Gona are being launched across the continent, while large-scale commercial farms are also boosting their scale and output. Between them, they could banish famine for Africa, turn the continent into a major agricultural exporter, and build powerful businesses all along the agriculture value chain—from fertilizers to farming, and from agri-technology to food processing. The prize will be shared by hundreds of millions of people, as agriculture is still by far the biggest source of employment in Africa.

African agriculture is attracting the attention of an increasingly global set of investors as well. One of them is Mitsui, the Japanese trading house, which announced in 2017 that it would pay some $265 million for a 30 percent stake in ETG, an African firm that is one of the world's largest traders of cashew nuts, pulses, and sesame seeds. Mitsui said its investment reflected the "major potential for growth in the African market."[42]

Such investments point to a big opportunity for agribusinesses able to innovate and apply best practices and technology to Africa's farm economy. The size of the opportunity is extraordinary. For example, McKinsey analyzed the potential to increase Africa's production of cereals, including rice, maize, millet, sorghum, and wheat. We found that the continent could more than quadruple its cereal production, principally by improving yields. That would take cereal production from 189 million tons in 2016 to more than 900 million tons in the future—enough to feed Africa's growing population *and* export to other regions. Africa could truly become the breadbasket of the world. At 2017 prices, this expanded production would be worth around $100 billion a year in additional income for African farmers. The upside in other crops could be just as dramatic.

Part of the opportunity lies in shifting African agriculture to higher-value crops. Kenya, for example, has tripled its horticulture exports to $700 million annually through such efforts. If we assume that higher-value products could replace 20 percent of Africa's low-value crops (such as cereal grains), agricultural production could rise by $140 billion annually by 2030. This shift would raise the incomes of Africa's millions of smallholder farmers. Morocco has already made great progress in this area: it is converting eleven hundred square miles of land from cereal to citrus-fruit and tomato cultivation, among other high-value crops.[43]

Private-sector companies and investment funds, which are already pouring serious money into African agriculture, have a central role to play in increasing the resources available to ignite and sustain a green revolution. Private-sector firms, both large and small, will also be at the heart of efforts to transform African agriculture on several key dimensions.

The first is to unlock technological breakthroughs. In particular, innovations are needed in developing new crop varietals, such as drought-tolerant maize, that would have high returns on investment and could sustainably raise small farmers from poverty. Cacao provides a good example. With global demand for chocolate forecast to grow steadily, food companies have sought to improve yields in West Africa, source of 70 percent of the world's cacao. Mars, the US-based food manufacturing giant, turned to genetics. Using its production base in Côte d'Ivoire, Mars publicly released the cacao tree genome that the company's agricultural research department mapped in partnership with the US Department of Agriculture and IBM in 2010. Not long after, Ivorian researchers released a quick-growing, more resilient variety named *cacao Mercedes*. Many local farmers are now selling more and better-quality beans, contributing to a

30 percent increase in Côte d'Ivoire's cacao production between 2012 and 2016.

Commercialization of such small-scale farming is a critical step, as 85 percent of Africa's farms occupy fewer than five acres—compared with only 11 percent in Brazil, for example. New industry models, like those of Babban Gona, can improve access to markets and help groups of small farmers raise their productivity.

Last, but not least, there is a critical need to scale up access to funding for Africa's farmers. By some estimates, sub-Saharan Africa alone requires additional annual investments of as much as $50 billion in its agriculture sector. African agriculture therefore needs business models that can significantly increase the level of investment from the private and public sectors, as well as donors—and translate that investment into impact. In Nigeria, for example, more than twenty banks worked with the government to design a $500 million risk-sharing facility to support lending to small and medium-sized agricultural businesses and producers.[44] Babban Gona is another innovation in agricultural financing: it is demonstrating that smallholder farmers are a viable target for investment and is helping to attract new capital to the sector.

RISING UP: NEW SOURCES OF GROWTH IN OIL AND GAS

In oil and gas, Africa is rich in high-potential regions, many of which remain unexplored. For example, the Rovuma Basin off the coast of Mozambique contains an estimated 180 trillion cubic feet of offshore gas—enough to supply Germany, the United Kingdom, France, and Italy for nearly two decades.[45]

When oil and gas prices began to fall sharply in 2014, there were questions about when and whether the world's oil majors would begin developing the field. That changed in June 2017, when Italy's Eni led a group that signed off on a $7 billion investment in a plant that, when complete, will export some 3.4 million tons a year of liquefied natural gas from Mozambique.[46] Eni's CEO, Claudio Descalzi, told us that the company is also setting its sights on selling more gas to African customers: "Africa represents 15 percent of the world's population, but uses 3 or 4 percent of worldwide energy. It has a lot of energy resources, but it doesn't have access to energy. That makes it a wonderful market."

We agree: McKinsey estimates that the domestic gas market in Africa will grow by 9 percent a year to 2025, propelled by the demands of power utilities, feedstock-based industries such as fertilizer, and captive generation. Even based on conservative per capita usage and growth, the continent could use up to 70 percent of its own gas. African countries could move away from the traditional extract-and-export model to one that makes better use of their resources on the continent.

Total, the France-based oil major, has made supplying Africa's growing markets a key pillar of its strategy—hence its focus on building the largest retail distribution network on the continent. It has also made a point of integrating into the forty-four African countries it operates in and ensuring it is a good corporate citizen. "Our mindset is to be very localized and part of the local context and community," said Patrick Pouyanné, its chairman and CEO. "Even our expatriate staff are expected to have multiyear life experiences with their families in our local markets, as opposed to operating on a rotation basis." Total is also investing heavily in building local talent and in raising its operational standards to global levels.

"We work with technically advanced processes and hazardous materials," Pouyanné told us, "So we have a responsibility to operate in every geography with the same high global standards, and to help propagate these standards in our communities." For example, the company has undertaken an extensive safety campaign to reduce fuel truck accidents and is proud of the zero-fatalities record it has achieved in recent years.

There are plenty of opportunities for other companies. Africa offers some of the world's most exciting hydrocarbon plays for oil-and-gas operators and investors alike. The continent is rich in unexplored, high-potential regions, including deepwater oil and onshore and offshore gas resources, which have gained particular notice.[47] Even in a global environment where oil and gas opportunities abound and there is much competition for capital, Africa is a continent to watch, both for its abundant resources and for the large unmet energy needs of its economies.

MINING: UNEARTHING AFRICA'S POTENTIAL

Along with oil and gas reserves, Africa also contains the world's largest reserves of vanadium, diamonds, manganese, phosphate, platinum-group metals, cobalt, aluminum, chromium, and gold. Only a fraction of Africa's subsoil assets has been discovered—as little as one-fifth the level of OECD countries, by some estimates.[48]

In January 2018, a UK-based mining company, Gem Diamonds, announced that it had recovered the fifth-largest diamond so far discovered—a 910-carat stone worth around $40 million—from its Letšeng mine in the Southern African nation of Lesotho. It wasn't a one-off find: since acquiring Letšeng in 2006, Gem Diamonds has discovered around sixty diamonds of more than one hundred carats each, including five of the twenty largest gem-quality diamonds ever recovered.[49]

That is a handy reminder of the spectacular riches hidden under Africa's soil. Eleven of its countries, especially in Southern and West Africa, rank among the top ten sources for at least one major mineral. The continent delivers some of the best value in the world for every dollar spent on exploration. Even so, mining has not been the consistent engine of economic development that people in many countries have hoped for. Nor, to date, has Africa attracted a share of global mining investment commensurate with its share of global resources. Of the five largest global diversified mining companies, only one has a major share of its production in Africa. Even outside well-publicized conflict zones, many African countries have been thought to pose high political and economic risks for investors. Moreover, infrastructure problems often hinder development: many bulk mineral deposits require multibillion-dollar investments in rail and port facilities to allow ore or semiprocessed minerals to reach their markets.

This combination of abundant resources and risk-wary investors has opened the way for entrepreneurial junior mining companies such as Gem Diamonds, as well as local African champions, to step up their role in developing the continent's resources. These players have been quick to spot global and African demand trends and ramp up their operations on the continent.

One such trend is the soaring demand for cobalt, a key component in electric-vehicle batteries. The volatile Democratic Republic of the Congo contains the world's largest cobalt reserves, and several junior mining companies have invested in exploration and production there. One of them, UK-based Sula Iron and Gold, announced in 2018 that it was changing its name to African Battery Metals to focus on the cobalt opportunity.[50]

Another mining trend is related to Africa's green revolution. Advances in Africa's agricultural production are increasing demand for fertilizers, for which phosphates, a mining commodity, are a key ingredient. Africa's current use of fertilizers, at twenty-six pounds per acre, is only one-quarter of the world average. One company responding to that demand is Morocco-based OCP, which has grown to become a global leader in phosphate mining and fertilizer production. It has made Africa its major growth market; in 2016, it increased its exports to the rest of the continent by 70 percent year-on-year.[51]

These examples underline the fact that, although Africa's economies have diversified significantly over the past two decades, mining remains a critically important sector in many countries. It is Africa's second-largest export industry, and accounts for 10 percent of the continent's GDP and foreign direct investment (FDI) inflows.[52] We expect demand for most of the major mined commodities to continue to grow over the next ten to twenty years. This provides ample opportunities for mining companies willing to act boldly and ride that wave of growth.

That said, the operating environment remains risky in many African countries. Mining companies can play their part in working with governments to improve it. One key step is to strengthen their "social license to operate" by investing in local communities, such as by microfinancing local enterprises or supporting educational institutions. For example, South Africa–based Randgold Resources established Community Development Committees (CDC) that enlist local leaders in community engagement. Each CDC manages a budget tied to a mine's production level and invests the budget in local development. In Mali, Randgold's investment in community development, including potable water and local agribusinesses, helped it to avoid being affected by the national strikes that hit other mining operations in 2014.[53]

TREND 5: RAPID ADOPTION OF DIGITAL AND MOBILE—AND THE LEAPFROG OPPORTUNITY

Technology adoption is a megatrend that could accelerate each of the trends we've highlighted in this chapter. In agriculture, for example, technology firms can lead the way in developing digital solutions that give farmers access to expertise and information on everything from weather, crop selection, and pest control to management and finance. They can also improve access to markets, generating better prices for produce. Other digital startups are helping farmers measure and analyze soil data so they can apply the right fertilizer and optimally irrigate their farms, and bringing them farming advice, weather forecasts, and financial tips.

Sara Menker, CEO of Gro Intelligence, envisages that these and other digital innovations will accelerate the commercialization of agriculture in Africa. "Even a small-scale farmer can start to produce specialty crops for the beauty industry rather than just corn to eat, for example," she told us. "On a per-acre basis, that will increase their income by multiples." Data-driven solutions can also help governments and private infrastructure investors focus new projects on where they're most needed. "If government can identify the hotspots of agricultural production, they can commit to building roads in those regions," Menker said.

There is much more room for such innovations. Sacha Poignonnec, CEO of Jumia, told us he was disappointed that the African technology sector remains much smaller than it could be, in part because it is underfunded. He hopes to see breakthrough growth in agricultural technology and solar power in particular: "Those are both areas where Africa has acute needs, and where technology has huge potential."

Jumia itself is proof that African technology firms can achieve real scale and attract the funding they need to do so. The company was launched by Rocket Internet, Germany's leading digital incubator, in 2012. Four years later it had become Africa's first technology "unicorn," with a valuation of over $1 billion. That was thanks in part to investments worth hundreds of millions of dollars from global firms such as Goldman Sachs, insurance company AXA, and mobile operators MTN and Orange. Today Jumia's marketplace platform offers consumers a vast range of products, from shoes to cell phones to generators, along with online services such as hotel bookings and restaurant deliveries.

Poignonnec told us that in most of the thirteen African countries Jumia operates in, about half its sales are to customers outside large cities, where access to formal retail is particularly limited. But Jumia is betting on rapid sales growth from urban and rural customers alike as e-commerce penetration ramps up. To encourage these habits, Jumia has created the JForce sales program, which has salespeople going door to door with Wi-Fi-connected tablets, taking orders from customers who lack internet access. "It allows agents to become entrepreneurs," Poignonnec said, "effectively operating their own online retail business right from home." Jumia has also created its own logistics service to fulfill its e-commerce orders; in 2017 it delivered 8 million packages. And it has built an in-house payment platform to help African consumers gain trust in online payments.

Research by McKinsey has demonstrated that internet-related services are a powerful catalyst for economic growth and social development.[54] In China, India, and Brazil, for example, the internet contributed more than 10 percent of total GDP growth over a recent five-year period, and its impact is accelerating. Our colleagues have found that an increase in a country's internet maturity correlates with a sizable increase in real per capita GDP.[55] As countries go online, they realize efficiencies in the delivery of public services and the operations of large and small businesses alike.

The benefits of internet-driven productivity gains are not limited to web-based companies: among small and medium-sized enterprises (SMEs), 75 percent of the economic impact of the internet has accrued to companies that are not pure internet players. In a global survey of forty-eight hundred SMEs, McKinsey found that across all sectors, companies utilizing web technologies grew more than twice as fast as those with a minimal online presence, generating more revenue through exports and creating more jobs. The internet also creates tremendous value for consumers. Online prices are, on average, around 10 percent lower than offline prices as a result of the transparency provided by search tools, generating tens of billions of dollars of consumer surplus in the nations with the widest internet use.[56]

Africa's internet penetration, however, lags behind other regions. Only 28 percent of the continent's 1 billion people were online in 2016—half the rate of the rest of the world. But that is changing fast: sub-Saharan Africa saw the world's fastest rate of new broadband connections between 2008 and 2015, at 34 percent per annum.[57] As noted earlier, mobile data traffic across Africa is expected to increase sevenfold between 2017 and 2022.[58]

To support this digital boom, major infrastructure expansions—from upgrading and installing submarine cables and backbone networks to various experiments to get rural and peri-urban Africa online—are under way. Several of the world's major technology companies, including Microsoft, Google, and Facebook, are investing in last-mile connectivity across the continent.[59] E-commerce in Africa is growing quickly: online retailers in Nigeria, for example, have experienced a doubling of revenue each year since 2010.[60]

Even in parts of Africa where internet access is still patchy or nonexistent, digital technology is changing the business landscape. Take electronic payments: there are already 122 million active users of mobile financial services in sub-Saharan Africa alone—more than in any other region of the world. More than one in ten sub-Saharan Africans has a mobile money account (figure 2-5). This number could grow exponentially if the rest of the continent follows the lead of East Africa, where virtually every adult holds a mobile money account.[61]

FIGURE 2-5

Africa is the world leader in mobile money

Active[1] mobile money accounts, 2017, million

121.9	86.3	18.3	11.5	7.2	1.7
Sub-Saharan Africa	South Asia	Middle East and N. Africa	Latin America and Caribbean	East Asia and Pacific	Europe and Central Asia

Adults[2] with mobile money account, 2017, %

20.9	4.2	5.8	5.3	1.3	3.2
Sub-Saharan Africa	South Asia	Middle East and N. Africa	Latin America and Caribbean	East Asia and Pacific	Europe and Central Asia

[1]Active for 90 days.
[2]Age 15 or over.

Source: GSMA Mobile Money Deployment Tracker; GSMA State of Industry Report 2016; World Bank Global Findex.

The economic impact of this acceleration could be proportionately greater in Africa than in other regions because the continent is in the relatively early stages of adoption of digital technologies. McKinsey's research shows that if Africa's businesses and governments harness the full economic potential of the internet, it could add $300 billion to the continent's GDP by 2025. The story of mobile telephony in Africa shows this projection is not far-fetched: cell phones have already had an outsized effect in Africa, connecting people who previously had little or no access to telecommunications due to the scarcity of fixed-line infrastructure.

Not only are innovative business models emerging across many of the largest sectors of Africa's economies, but existing companies are streamlining processes, speeding up transactions, tightening supply-chain management, and accessing wider markets. New tools are available to make a leap forward in the quality and availability of health care, education, and public services. If Africa accelerates its adoption of digital and mobile technologies, it will realize major productivity gains, which in turn will translate into higher living standards and greater business opportunities across the continent.

Africa is changing fast. Its cities are growing upward and outward at a remarkable pace, its young population is enthusiastically buying brands and adopting new technologies, and those same technologies are opening the way for breakthrough solutions to long-standing challenges ranging from electric power to education. None of these trends is linear, and each comes with its fair share of twists—but if you can figure out a strategy to ride one or more of them, you could build a very fast-growing business in Africa. How will you do it? In part 2 of this book we share our own views—and those of some of the continent's most successful businesspeople—on what it takes to win in Africa.

PART TWO

HOW TO WIN
IN AFRICA

A STRATEGIC GUIDE

CHAPTER 3

MAP YOUR AFRICA STRATEGY

If, like us, your work keeps you traveling across Africa, you end up spending a lot of time on planes. A direct flight from Cairo to Johannesburg takes eight hours—longer than the trip from New York to Paris. Getting from Nairobi in East Africa to Accra in West Africa will take you six hours, the equivalent of a flight between the East and West coasts of the United States. If you go the overland route, you should plan on a bit longer: when a colleague of ours decided to motorcycle from Cape Town on the southern tip of Africa to Egypt in the north, he ended up taking six months.

If any of these distances surprise you, you're not alone. Many people underestimate just how big Africa is. In part, that's the fault of the commonly used Mercator mapping system, which has the effect of shrinking regions on and around the equator and magnifying those closer to the poles. In reality, Africa is larger than the United States, China, India, Japan, and much of Europe combined (figure 3-1). Africa's land area, at 11 million square miles, is second only to Asia's.

FIGURE 3-1

Africa is bigger than you think: it dwarfs China, India, Europe, and the United States

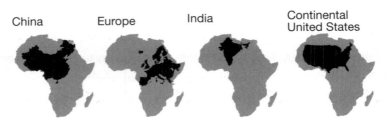

Source: Kai Krause, "The True Size of Africa," http://kai.sub.blue/images/True-Size-of-Africa-kk-v3.pdf.

Africa contains a few highly populated countries: Nigeria has nearly 190 million people; Ethiopia, 93 million; and Egypt, 92 million. But most African nations have populations below 20 million—fewer inhabitants than the US state of Florida. The same is true of GDP: just nine countries make up three-quarters of Africa's GDP, although many smaller countries are growing fast. To serve a sizeable market, companies must therefore shape a coherent geographic portfolio that prioritizes the countries or cities they will play in.

In other words, you need to map your Africa strategy. If your map is to serve as a meaningful guide on your journey of business growth, it will have to be fact-based and granular—at the hundred-foot, not ten-thousand-foot scale. You will have to dispense with generalizations, and truly understand the differences in countries' wealth, growth, and risk profiles.

Each company's strategic map of Africa will be unique, influenced by the customers it seeks to serve, the opportunities in its industry, and whether it has strengths or local knowledge in a particular country or region. Your map might be focused on a few countries in which you invest to build a leading position—or even a single large market such as Nigeria. You might expand country by country to build a regional business—say, in East Africa or Francophone West Africa. Or you might go much broader and create a pan-African conglomerate.

Saham Finances has put itself firmly in the "expand your map" camp. In little over a decade, the Morocco-based company grew from a small local firm into a leading African insurance company operating in twenty-three countries across the continent. Between 2005 and 2015, it increased its sales nearly tenfold, to over $1 billion. Nadia Fettah, the company's CEO, is one of the few women at the helm of a major African business. "Our first step was to become a big player in Morocco, which we succeeded to do in three or four years," she told us. "But our ambition was big and our market was small, so we looked for the next countries to expand into. We considered North Africa and Europe, but when we started traveling in sub-Saharan Africa, we realized that we could have major impact there: most countries had very low insurance penetration. There was big potential to serve clients who had very little access to insurance."

Saham embarked on a bold strategy of buying stakes in existing insurance firms in countries ranging from Angola to Madagascar, then overhauling their management and rapidly growing their sales. In 2016, Saham took its African expansion strategy to the next level: it partnered with Sanlam, a long-established South African insurance company that had also made Africa its major growth focus. "They were moving north, we were moving south; we met in the middle," Fettah recounted. "Together we have the biggest footprint of any insurance company in Africa, covering thirty-four countries." That partnership turned into a merger in 2018, when Sanlam announced a full acquisition of Saham in a transaction that valued the Morocco-based insurer at $2 billion. In a vote of confidence, Sanlam said it would keep Fettah on as CEO of Saham. (Shortly afterwards, Africa's top CEO forum named her CEO of the year.) Fettah's erstwhile colleagues in Casablanca won't just be pocketing the proceeds of the sale: Saham's parent group announced its transformation into a pan-African investment fund focused on "future-oriented businesses" across the continent.[1] Its aim is to replicate its success in insurance in other growth sectors.

African-owned businesses are not the only ones pursuing bold geographic expansion. According to a McKinsey analysis, eighty-eight large multinationals operating in Africa had built pan-African businesses with operations in more than ten countries. Nearly a third of them are present in more than twenty countries, and on average, the firms with the widest footprint have the largest revenues. For these multinationals, drawing a pan-African map has typically been a decades-long undertaking: most have been in the continent for twenty-five years or more (figure 3-2).

Coca-Cola is arguably the most pan-African multinational of all. Whether you're in a village in rural Mali or a street market in bustling Kampala, you'll find a Coke to quench your thirst— or another of the dozens of brands the company has tailored to local markets, such as Stoney Tangawizi ginger-flavored soft drink in East Africa. That is the result of a clear vision articulated at the beginning of this century: to make sure

FIGURE 3-2

For most multinationals, building a pan-African business is a decades-long undertaking

Most large multinationals have been in Africa for 25 years or more.

More than half of large multinationals are present in more than 10 countries.

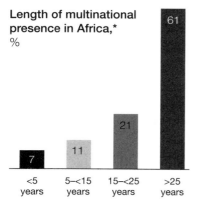

Length of multinational presence in Africa,*
%

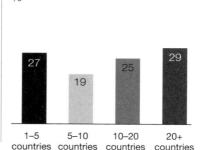

Countries of multinationals' presence in Africa,*
%

*Sample size determined by data availability; only multinationals with African revenue of $500 million or more were analyzed.

Source: MGI African Companies Database; McKinsey Global Institute analysis.

there's a Coca-Cola beverage in reach of every consumer who wants one. The company had long been present in Africa, but in 2000 Coca-Cola's board decided to make the continent a priority for growth. Its rationale was clear: Africa's population was growing fast, yet its per capita consumption of Coca-Cola products was less than 1 percent of that in North America, and much smaller than in other emerging markets.

Liberian-born Alex Cummings was appointed president of Coca-Cola's Africa Group in 2001 after leading its Nigerian operations. He gave us the inside track on the company's daring Africa expansion strategy. Eager to grow its presence in emerging markets, Coca-Cola let its Africa leadership team take risks and make bets that other companies might have balked at. For example, it opened a $26 million bottling plant in Angola in 2000, while the country was in the middle of a civil war. "People thought we were crazy," said Cummings, "but today we're selling around 40 million cases a year in that market."

Likewise, the company acquired a bottling plant in Zimbabwe in 2004, when the country was in the midst of hyperinflation and recession and other multinationals were leaving. "We thought: at some point this country will turn, and when it does we want to be there," Cummings told us. Coca-Cola even opened a new bottling plant in Somalia during his tenure. "My colleagues went in, flak jackets and all," said Cummings. "It was important to show Somalis that the world had not abandoned them."

Companies like Coca-Cola and Saham, along with successful firms that have chosen to concentrate on a smaller African footprint, provide four navigation tools to master Africa's geographical complexity and draw the right strategic map for profitable growth:

1. Set a clear aspiration to guide your expansion strategy.

2. Prioritize the markets that matter most for your business.

3. Define how you'll achieve scale and relevance across your African map.

4. Identify—and help build—the ecosystem you need to thrive.

NAVIGATION TOOL 1: SET A CLEAR ASPIRATION TO GUIDE YOUR EXPANSION STRATEGY

For Coca-Cola, the answer to "Which country?" was every country in Africa, regardless of political or economic stability. "We thought about Africa holistically and took a long view," said Alex Cummings. "We had a clear vision and strong belief in what we could build in Africa—and that was backed up with facts. But we knew it wouldn't be simple, and that there'd be peaks and valleys on our growth journey. We knew from the start that we'd have to be tenacious."

The company invested billions of dollars in building its network of bottlers and salespeople, buying up local beverage companies, and strengthening its African organization. As a result, Coca-Cola increased its Africa volumes by over 50 percent in less than a decade and grew revenues and profits even faster. Coca-Cola and its bottling partners today employ seventy thousand people across Africa, making it one of the largest private-sector employers on the continent. Those achievements propelled Cummings to the role of global chief administrative officer, based at Coca-Cola's Atlanta headquarters, until his retirement in 2016. (It hasn't been a quiet retirement: Cummings ran for president of Liberia in 2017.)

Likewise, Saham set out a bold, continentwide vision from the start. "Our goal was to become the best insurance company in Africa," CEO Nadia Fettah told us. That led the company to expand quickly across different regions of Africa. First it built a presence in the Francophone countries of West Africa—which made life easier for its Moroccan managers, all of whom speak French. "But we also wanted to go to other big markets in Africa that were underpenetrated," Fettah said. "So we went to Angola and became the first private insurance company there. We also invested in Nigeria, Kenya, Rwanda, Madagascar, and Mauritius." Despite language and cultural differences, Saham built successful businesses in all these markets, creating lean, highly empowered local leadership teams backed by shared, technology-driven back-office systems.

Rapid expansion often comes with challenges, as the example of Saham's entry into Angola illustrates. It bought a fast-growing local insurance company in 2015, but just as the deal closed, the oil price collapsed and put Angola's oil-dependent economy into a tailspin. "Suddenly, everything went wrong," Fettah told us. "We were facing a crisis. But we took a long-term view, and our local management team quickly came up with a strategy to save the business." Rather than scaling back, Saham focused on ramping up sales to business customers, including thousands of smaller enterprises. Within a year, its Angolan business had returned to profitability and built a real beachhead for the company. "As we were growing, our competitors were halting their investments," said Fettah. "That will give us a strong competitive advantage when the economy recovers."

At about the same time Saham set its sights on becoming a pan-African business, another Moroccan financial services firm did the same. Attijariwafa Bank was running up against the limits to growth in its home market, and in 2005 it set the goal of becoming a pan-African bank. It understood that while banking penetration in Morocco was deep, that was not the case in many of the countries it hoped to expand to. Rather than limit itself to a small, upper slice of the market, Attijariwafa embraced a new role as the institution that would bring banking services to informal companies and individuals who did not bank. By 2017, Attijariwafa was the sixth-largest bank in Africa, with operations in twenty-five countries across the continent and beyond.

BROAD OR NARROW?

Of course, a pan-African map is not the only recipe for success. Among the large companies in our survey sample (those with annual revenues exceeding $1 billion), around one-third are pan-African firms with operations in more than ten countries, another third operate in four to ten countries, and the remaining third operate in one to three African countries. That picture is anything but static, however. Nearly half these large firms report that the number of countries they operate in has increased over the past five years, and most of them plan further geographic expansion over the next five years. Hardly any intend to shrink their African footprint. Smaller firms, though they are, unsurprisingly, present in fewer countries today, are just as ambitious in their expansion plans.

These findings are consistent with analysis undertaken by McKinsey on the expansion strategies of Africa's hundred largest and most successful companies.[2] (We picked these "top 100" from the database of large companies described in chapter 2, using both published company information where it was available, and the insights of our colleagues working across the continent.) We got a rich sense of how winning businesses have expanded their African footprints over multiple decades. The large majority of these companies grew big by developing a strong position in their home market first. As they grew in scale, though, they drew their maps differently: half of them remained focused on one of Africa's larger markets, while the other half steadily expanded to become regional or pan-African companies.

Several of the companies we looked at in the course of writing this book explained that they were deliberately keeping their geographic focus narrow. For example, Tayo Oviosu, CEO of the mobile payments startup Paga, said, "We're not planning to expand beyond Nigeria at this stage; Nigeria is a very big market and we have a long road ahead of us here." It's a sound decision: Paga grew its customer base from nothing to 8 million in just a few years, but its potential market in Nigeria is many times that number.

The scale of your geographic expansion will in part be determined by your sector. Among respondents to our executive survey, more than 60 percent of retail and consumer goods companies plan to expand into additional African countries over the next five years, while fewer than 40 percent of financial services companies plan to do the same. Indeed, our research suggests that broad-based regional expansion has not always resulted in better performance in the banking sector. On average, banks with significant regional or pan-African footprints have underperformed the "national champions" focused on their home markets. We analyzed twenty-six national champions and found that their revenue grew at a compound annual rate of 20 percent between 2011 and 2016, while their average ROE in 2016 stood at 13 percent. Among the thirteen regional banks we studied, however, annual revenue growth was 14 percent and ROE in 2016 was just 8 percent.[3] It is clear that companies in complex, highly regulated sectors such as banking must be careful in their choice of where to compete, and then be sure they have what it takes to go head-to-head with established local players.

EMPOWER TO EXPAND

That said, there is also a danger that you could be too conservative in your expansion strategy and let more aggressive competitors, like Coca-Cola and Saham, build a strong position in markets that look risky today but could be fast-growing tomorrow. Western firms are often more cautious than their African counterparts—and more risk-averse than the Chinese companies that are expanding rapidly across the continent. We found that around 70 percent of African- and Chinese-headquartered companies are planning to expand their footprint in Africa in the next few years, compared with barely 40 percent of North American firms.

As just one example of Chinese firms' ambition in Africa, consider the CGCOC Group. This giant construction firm started its African business drilling boreholes in Nigeria, then expanded both up and down the value chain and geographically across the continent. As of 2017, it had subsidiaries in twenty-four African countries. Its businesses span real estate, manufacturing, green energy, agriculture, and mining. At the time of writing, it had more than 250 active projects—ranging from a water supply project near Douala, Cameroon, to a wind power project near Addis Ababa.

When we met one of CGCOC's senior managers, Huang Shiyi, in Beijing, he attributed the company's rapid expansion to its willingness to move fast to seize opportunities, and its readiness to partner with both African governments and Western financial institutions. Indeed, many of its current projects are funded by Western banks and agencies. Just like Coca-Cola's, CGCOC's bold expansion strategy has been enabled by a head office that's been willing to let its Africa business take some risks. "That's the best thing that ever happened to us," Huang said. "We've pretty much always met our profit targets, so our shareholders in China have left us alone to make calls on the ground. That's been a huge business advantage—you can't work in a developing country and expect to always be able to ask HQ."

Nadia Fettah of Saham echoes that sentiment: "We have a large portfolio of businesses in smaller countries, so we at headquarters can't micromanage. Instead, we give our country managers a lot of freedom, and make sure the people we appoint to those roles are real entrepreneurs." Saham issues guidelines on management and provides its country operations with technology-driven back-office support. "Beyond that," Fettah says, "we let our local operations decide what to do and how to do it." She gives the example of Burkina Faso, one of Africa's smallest and poorest countries. Thanks to the energy and ideas of Saham's local country manager, who targeted underserved business customers, it has become one of Saham's fastest-growing markets.

You might be skeptical about Burkina Faso as your next growth market. But there is one more reason to make your African map broad rather than narrow: the need to diversify risk. This is a theme we return to in chapter 5. For now, it's worth quoting an executive at a global resources company, who told us frankly: "We operate in around thirty countries in Africa. We know that every year as many as five of those countries will blow up, but the other twenty-five will do great. And for more than twenty years, we have done very well in Africa." Our experience backs that up. We observe that, once companies have succeeded in three to five African countries, expansion becomes easier and risk typically diminishes. In a larger, diversified geographical portfolio, an unexpected political or financial shock in one country can be offset by businesses elsewhere.

NAVIGATION TOOL 2: PRIORITIZE THE MARKETS THAT MATTER MOST FOR YOUR BUSINESS

In a continent with Africa's scale and geographic complexity, you need to be ruthless in prioritizing the markets in which you will focus your investments and management attention. Again, Coca-Cola provides a compelling example. Even though it is present across the continent, it has not taken a one-size-fits-all approach to Africa's diverse markets. On the contrary, Alex Cummings's leadership team weighed up the market size and growth prospects of all fifty-four countries and picked ten as priorities for growth—Egypt, Ethiopia, Ghana, Kenya, Morocco, Mozambique, Nigeria, South Africa, Tanzania, and Uganda. Within each of those countries, Coca-Cola focused on the big cities that accounted for the lion's share of GDP, such as Lagos, Abuja, and Port Harcourt in Nigeria. "A big-city strategy made practical sense," said Cummings, "because with many of our bottlers using returnable glass bottles, cities were just easier to get to."

But what of the forty-four African countries and thousands of smaller towns that were *not* on Coca-Cola's priority list?

In smaller countries, the company offered a much simpler port-folio of products and packaging. In Cummings's native Liberia, for example, the company until recently sold its sparkling beverages only in returnable glass bottles. In its priority African markets, on the other hand, it also offers the cans and plastic bottles familiar to Western consumers and produces a broader choice of brands, such as Dasani water and Minute Maid juices.

BET ON TOMORROW'S GROWTH MARKETS, NOT TODAY'S

As Coca-Cola's experience suggests, the construction of a successful African portfolio depends heavily on picking the right countries. But that is often the starting point. Companies considering setting up business in Africa need to look not just at the spending power of countries today, but also at how their growth trajectories differ. For instance, annual GDP per capita ranges from around $10,000 in middle-income South Africa and Tunisia to $1,500 in Kenya and Zambia to less than $500 in the DRC. Africa contains some of the world's fastest-growing economies, including Ethiopia, which grew its GDP at a compound annual growth rate of nearly 10 percent between 2014 and 2017.[4] Countries such as Côte d'Ivoire, Ghana, Rwanda, and Tanzania have been growing nearly as fast. But two of Africa's largest economies, Nigeria and South Africa, have seen growth slow in recent years. As a result, demand patterns are shifting: we expect East Africa and Francophone Central and West Africa to increase their share of Africa's overall consumption significantly by 2025, while South Africa's share will fall. Nigeria remains an essential component in most African portfolios: it represents nearly a quarter of the continent's total consumer spending (figure 3-3).

FIGURE 3-3

Consumption is growing much faster in some parts of Africa than others

Total household consumption by region, %, $ billion, 2015 prices

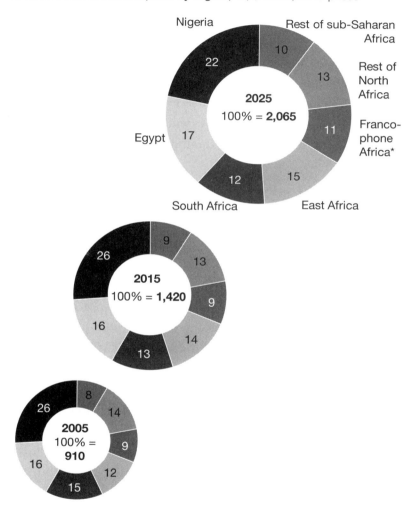

*Includes 15 countries in Central and West Africa; excludes North Africa and East Africa.

Source: Oxford Economics: IHS; African Development Bank; McKinsey Global Institute analysis.

Our executive survey suggests there is a next generation of African growth markets that are catching the attention of local companies, but that are still largely off foreign-based multinationals' radar screens. These rising stars include Côte d'Ivoire, Ethiopia, and Ghana. Africa-based executives were twice as likely as their international counterparts to name these as top-priority countries. Conversely, nearly half of non-African respondents said South Africa was the country offering their company the biggest growth opportunities, but just 27 percent of African respondents agreed. As you draw your map of Africa, we suggest you take that as a reminder to focus on tomorrow's markets, not just today's.

THINK CITIES, NOT JUST COUNTRIES

Coca-Cola's decision to prioritize major cities while maintaining a lighter-touch approach to reach consumers in rural villages makes a lot of sense: "Think cities, not countries" should be a mantra when working out where and how to win in Africa. As we pointed out in chapter 1, Africa's population is expected to almost double by 2050. As it does so, more than 80 percent of that growth will occur in cities.[5] Each year for the next twenty years, an average of 24 million Africans will move to cities. By the end of the next decade, Africa will have nearly ninety cities with at least a million inhabitants. The number of cities with more than 5 million inhabitants will more than double, from six to seventeen. The population of Lagos, Africa's fastest-growing city, is increasing by an astonishing seventy-seven people every hour, according to United Nations data.[6]

Rapid urbanization is one good reason why consumer-facing companies should make cities a central focus of their African growth strategies. But there's a second good reason: Africa's urban dwellers have much higher incomes than their rural cousins. In fact, per capita consumption in Africa's large cities is nearly double the average of these cities' host countries. In Nairobi, and in the Nigerian cities of Abuja, Ibadan, Lagos, and Port Harcourt, per capita consumption is close to three times the national average. The largest three cities in Angola and Ghana account for more than 65 percent of national consumption. Indeed, Africa's overall consumer spending is highly concentrated in a small number of urban centers—just seventy-five cities across Africa account for nearly half of the continent's total consumption. As urbanization progresses, their share of spending will only increase.[7]

RESOURCES: CHOOSE THE RIGHT SPACE TO WIN

Companies in the resources sector will need to map the potential and ease of extraction of the relevant commodities. For mining companies and oil and gas players, this task is made all the more complex by the sheer scale of the minerals opportunity across the continent and by the fact that such a large proportion of Africa's mineral resources is still to be discovered. As we discussed in part 1, the growth in oil and gas in particular will come from an increasingly diverse group of nations. Companies in the agriculture value chain will need a clear understanding of the distribution and productiveness of Africa's cropland and how that will be affected by factors such as climate change. Such companies need to locate where there are resources, but they also need to understand how the regulatory environment and competitive landscape is shifting in each market they operate in.

Consider the example of SIFCA in Côte d'Ivoire. In partnership with France's Michelin, it has become one of the world's largest natural rubber producers, with plantations and industrial plants not just in its home country but also in Ghana, Liberia, and Nigeria. It has also achieved a leading position in palm oil, for which there is rising demand across Africa. In that commodity, it has developed major plantations, along with Africa's biggest palm oil refinery, in Côte d'Ivoire. From there, it exports the oil across West Africa. It has also partnered with Singapore-based Wilmar International to grow and refine palm oil in Ghana, and is planning to expand production into Nigeria.

Yet SIFCA was once a major player in cacao, too, but had to exit that commodity when global players like US-based Cargill ramped up their presence in West Africa. SIFCA's former CEO, Jean-Louis Billon, told us: "Côte d'Ivoire used to be a fairly protected market, but liberalization brought in the big players and pushed down the cacao price. We just couldn't compete, and in 2000, we recorded our biggest-ever loss." That chastening experience has guided SIFCA's approach to constructing its country and commodity map ever since. The company has carefully chosen the places and products where it can be big enough to compete and has found strong global partners to bolster its position. "When you have a partner that's active on the international market, that makes things much easier," said Billon. "While our international partners have benefited from our local knowledge, we have benefited from their expertise." For example, SIFCA's partnership with Wilmar boosted the output of its palm oil plants considerably.

NAVIGATION TOOL 3: DEFINE HOW YOU'LL ACHIEVE SCALE AND RELEVANCE ACROSS YOUR AFRICAN MAP

Drawing your company's map is a first important step in building a winning business in Africa—but you also need a clear plan for how you will achieve relevance, scale, and customer loyalty in every territory you play in. As the experience of Coca-Cola shows, there are a few essential components to that plan.

The first is your brand. "African consumers are as brand conscious as consumers anywhere," Alex Cummings says. Because African consumers and businesses must navigate greater uncertainty in their daily lives than their counterparts in developed markets do, they place great value on brands they can trust. As Cummings emphasized: "We wanted to make it totally clear that our brand was something they could rely on, and that we were here for good." That philosophy helped the Coca-Cola Africa team make some tough decisions. In the DRC, for example, a bottler wanted to put Coke in standard plastic bottles instead of the company's iconic curved ones, to make the beverage more affordable. Coca-Cola answered with a flat no. "We insisted that our brand standards were the same everywhere," said Cummings. "The notion that a lower-spec package was 'good enough for Africa' really irritated me."

A much harder test came when the Ebola epidemic hit the West African nations of Guinea, Liberia, and Sierra Leone in 2014. The disease not only took thousands of lives, it also devastated those countries' economies—and Coca-Cola's businesses. "When everyone else was running away, I got onto a company jet with my colleagues and headed to Liberia and Guinea," recalls Cummings. "It was important that people saw we were committed." Although sales were down by 60 percent, the company made sure that all of its employees were paid their salary on time, and were trained to avoid getting infected with Ebola. Not one of them contracted the disease. Coca-Cola also contributed water and drinks, medical equipment and supplies, and financial support to community relief efforts.

As these stories suggest, Coca-Cola's success in making its brand so widely loved in Africa has been underpinned by deep commitment on the part of its executives: Cummings recruited a leadership team that was 75 percent African. "We knew more about the continent than anyone else, we had passion, and we cared," he told us. That rubbed off on the company's hundreds of millions of customers across the continent. Cummings recalls a party the company organized to celebrate its fiftieth anniversary in Kenya. A young man approached him and asked in all seriousness: "Is Coke sold in America too?" To Cummings, that was a sign that Coke had truly become a local product. "That was when I knew that our African customers had really taken ownership of the brand," he told us.

Building off that brand strength, Coca-Cola embarked on a second key step: tailoring its offering to Africa's diverse consumers, country by country and city by city. (We explore this theme in more depth in chapter 4.) In the company's priority African markets, it conducted a careful customer segmentation exercise, then both evolved its traditional products and created new ones to target each segment. In Lagos's low-income neighborhoods, for example, it sold Coke in returnable glass bottles at low prices. For middle-income consumers who shop in supermarkets, Coke was sold in plastic bottles and cans, which across the continent are seen as higher status and come at a premium.

That same differentiation extended to its portfolio of brands. Some, like Stoney Tangawizi, are carbonated soft drinks targeted to local taste. Others, like its growing range of fruit juices and waters, are aimed at Africans who are following global wellness trends. "There is more money in Africa than many people realize," said Cummings. "Categories like juices might not be big volume drivers but they will be big profit drivers, as they have healthy margins."

The third key step was to expand Coca-Cola's on-the-ground presence in its markets—through acquisitions, partnerships, or a combination of the two. Once it had identified its priority Africa countries, Coca-Cola took a hard look at its existing partnership network: in Morocco, for example, it changed its bottler. In other markets, achieving greater local relevance and scale meant acquiring new brands and facilities, setting the pace for a buying spree that continues to this day. In 2016, for example, Coca-Cola announced it was paying $240 million for a stake in Nigerian juice and dairy company CHI.[8]

Depending on your industry and your starting point, you too will need to determine how to play across your African map. To achieve rapid pan-African scale, Saham chose to become a serial acquirer of small insurance firms across the continent. Another firm, Liquid Telecom, has become the largest pan-African broadband infrastructure and data services company, with more than thirty thousand miles of fiber across twelve countries, through both organic growth and acquisitions. It has been willing to pay real money to build scale: in 2017, it bought South Africa's Neotel for some $430 million.[9]

NAVIGATION TOOL 4: IDENTIFY, AND HELP BUILD, THE ECOSYSTEM YOU NEED TO THRIVE

Your strategic map of Africa should also highlight the places where you have strong partners who can help you succeed—and those where you'll need to invest in building out your business ecosystem. The guiding question here is: *Who will we work with to win?* Your ecosystem must be broad enough to provide all the elements you need to run your business in Africa. These include reliable power and water supply, appropriately sited land, a robust supplier base for everything from raw materials to business services, and a distribution network that can get your product into towns and villages across the continent.

For global businesses investing in Africa, the trick is often to find local partners who understand the lay of the land. That has been the approach of many of the multinationals featured in this book. One example, cited earlier, is Singapore-based Wilmar, whose partnership with Côte d'Ivoire's SIFCA has created highly successful palm oil operations. Another, discussed in chapter 4, is the US-based Kellogg, which views Africa as a key growth market but needed local expertise to market and distribute its food products to African consumers. It partnered with Nigeria-based Tolaram Africa, which is also the West African distributor for Denmark-based Arla Foods, one of the world's largest dairy companies.[10] These Western consumer-goods firms benefit not just from Tolaram's tried-and-tested sales and logistics infrastructure, but also its integrated supply chain and close relationships with African governments.

Even companies with a close knowledge of Africa need a robust ecosystem of local partners—and pay the price if that ecosystem is found wanting. One example is South Africa's Public Investment Corporation (PIC), which manages the pension funds of the country's civil servants. It invested hundreds of millions of dollars in firms in other African countries, but saw some of those investments run into trouble. CEO Dan Matjila told us that had been "a real eye-opener." He explained: "We found out later that some of the domestic companies we mandated to conduct due diligence didn't dig deep enough to uncover some of the issues we are dealing with post-investment." Matjila remains convinced that Africa outside his home country remains a promising bet: "We're not retreating. We're shaping a different partnership approach. We realize now that we have to be present on the ground in the countries in our portfolio, and active inside the companies we invest in, with a real seat at the table. That makes us much better able to detect and manage risk."

As that example suggests, selecting the right partners is not enough. You also need a smart way to mobilize them around your business objectives. Again, Coca-Cola provides a compelling illustration of the approach needed. "You can find a Coke in every village in Africa," Alex Cummings is proud to affirm. To achieve that feat, the company relied on its bottler, distributor, and retail partners and designed the economics so that each one of them was incentivized to get its products into consumers' hands. "Everyone made a buck along the way, so we could rely on our distribution network to cover the rural areas while we focused on the cities," Cummings told us.

Other multinationals have adopted similar approaches to distribution—and supported the emergence of a cohort of African entrepreneurs skilled at "last mile" delivery of beverages, pharmaceuticals, cleaning products, cigarettes, and a host of other consumer goods. One of them is Kenya-based Kaskazi Network. Its founder, Ng'ang'a Wanjohi, recognized a business opportunity in Africa's tangled city centers and remote rural areas, where residents shop almost entirely at hard-to-reach informal shops and kiosks. Kaskazi's five hundred sales representatives deliver goods via motorcycle from fast-moving consumer goods companies to informal shops and kiosks across Kenya. Supply is only part of Kaskazi's value proposition. Its sales reps also become a vital source of market intelligence, feeding back insights on competition and counterfeiters, tips on promotions, and information on why products are moving quickly or slowly.[11]

As we pointed out in chapter 2, poor connectivity in many of Africa's cities means that businesses, particularly manufacturers, can struggle to find reliable suppliers and other partners to build and sustain large-scale businesses. As Oxford University economist Paul Collier explained it to us: "The miracle of productivity is driven by scale and specialization. And the two go together, because the more scale you've got, the more specialization is feasible." That, he emphasized, requires clusters of connected, efficient firms. "In order to achieve scale and specialization, you need a lot more connectivity than if you're just operating solo," he says. Collier's thesis is that the "congested sprawl" of African cities has hampered the development of clusters, which in part explains why Africa has been slow to break into global manufacturing. Scarce availability of industrial land, he added, just deepens this problem: "Land markets are probably the most important thing that's gone wrong in African cities."

As you build your own ecosystem, you need to think carefully about how to get around these obstacles. One approach is to pick the cities and countries where connectivity is strongest and efficient clusters of suppliers and business partners are forming. Donald Kaberuka, former president of the African Development Bank, points to his native Rwanda as one such country. Excellent transport, easily navigable regulations, and major focus by government on education and training have made the East African nation a natural business cluster. "In Rwanda, we have built businesses around other businesses," Kaberuka told us. "We are building a value chain that one day could support big companies like Boeing."

Another approach is to locate your business in one of Africa's growing number of greenfield industrial hubs—several of which are being built away from major urban centers in partnership between governments and business. Hawassa in Ethiopia (see chapter 2) is one of those. Ethiopia's strategy to create a global apparel manufacturing hub in this once-sleepy backwater appears to be working, backed as it is by infrastructure investments in airports, highways, and a modern rail link to the Port of Djibouti. (In fact, as Donald Kaberuka points out, Ethiopia and Djibouti are "the extension of one region" for manufacturers.) A McKinsey survey conducted in 2017 found that large global apparel companies see Ethiopia as the most attractive country for future sourcing opportunities—ahead of Asian competitors such as Bangladesh and Vietnam.[12]

There are several other established industry clusters that bring together suppliers, enabling infrastructure, and skilled workers. In Morocco, for example, Tangier is home to a thriving free-trade zone established as part of a government-backed industrial plan launched in the early 2000s. The cornerstone of this plan has been the creation of export-focused special economic zones supplied with top-quality infrastructure and located close to major ports. Morocco offers significant financial incentives to manufacturers who invest in these zones, including exemption from corporate tax for the first five years (and a flat tax rate of 8.75 percent for the next twenty years), as well as exemptions from customs duties, value-added tax, and local and personnel taxes.

Today Tanger Automotive City is home to more than thirty multinationals—including a $1 billion Renault auto plant. In 2016, Renault produced more than 270,000 vehicles at the plant and employed around eight thousand workers. The plant gives Renault access to both Europe and Morocco, where its brands have a leading position in the market. It is also a gateway to the rest of North Africa. Tanger Automotive City has become a training center and a center for research into next-generation digital technology as the companies that have located there compete with, supply, and collaborate with one another.[13]

Of course, not all centrally planned hubs take off, and companies considering locating within them need to carefully evaluate their potential. In particular, Africa's experience with special economic zones (SEZs), which typically provide simplified access to land and infrastructure along with favorable labor and trade regulations, has been disappointing. The World Bank has described African SEZs as "underperforming" compared with their Asian and Latin American counterparts.[14] African nations have too often followed the "build it and see what comes" approach to SEZ development. Zones targeted at and tailored for a specific cluster of industries—like Tanger Automotive City and Hawassa—have been much more successful.[15] You need to tread carefully in picking a hub that truly supports your business growth.

We should emphasize that not all successful hubs are government-planned. In your search for an ecosystem to support your business, you should also weigh up the industry clusters that have developed informally. In Kenya, for example, a thriving information and communication technology sector has grown up around Nairobi's Ngong Road. iHub, an incubator and co-working space in the heart of Nairobi, has supported some hundred tech startups over the past seven years.[16] One such is iCow, an app to help farmers track and manage poultry, livestock, and other aspects of their business. On the other end of the spectrum, IBM operates a $10 million research lab in Nairobi. Google, Microsoft, and Intel also have operations in the city.

Africa's rapidly growing local and national economies offer enormous opportunities. As companies consider entering those markets or expanding across the continent, they need to carefully craft a geographic portfolio strategy that takes into consideration current and future conditions, as well as the rapidly evolving competitive landscape. Choosing the cities and countries to compete in is just the starting point in mapping your Africa strategy. You also need a clear plan to build scale and local relevance in your African markets, and to find the partners who will help you win in each of them.

CHAPTER 4

INNOVATE YOUR BUSINESS MODEL

Kellogg, the US-based food manufacturing company, made headlines in 2015 when it invested $450 million in Tolaram Africa, a Nigeria-based company that few in the West had heard of. Kellogg's chairman and CEO John Bryant announced a long-term partnership and a 50 percent stake in Tolaram's West African sales and distribution company. At the time, he said, "As a region that is experiencing explosive growth, sub-Saharan Africa provides tremendous opportunity for our company. Tolaram Africa has built a highly successful consumer products business, and today it is one of the largest food companies in Nigeria. This partnership is an excellent strategic fit for Kellogg."[1]

To understand what Kellogg gets from this alliance, consider the remarkable story of Tolaram's crown jewel, the humble Indomie brand of instant noodles, today one of Nigeria's most beloved consumer products. Sold in single-serving packets for the equivalent of less than 20 US cents, the brand enjoys near-universal name recognition and has attracted a 150,000-member fan club. The brand is so well woven into Nigerian society that it might surprise Nigerians to recall that noodles are not among their traditional foods and that Tolaram has operated in the country for just thirty years.[2] (The company's origins are in Asia; its parent company is headquartered in Singapore.)

Dufil Prima Foods, the Tolaram company that produces Indomie noodles, introduced the product in Nigeria in 1988. At the time, the country was under military rule, per capita income was barely $250, and four out of five Nigerians lived on less than $2 a day. But in these circumstances, the company saw an opportunity to feed a nation with an affordable and convenient product—and in so doing, create a new category. The vast majority of Nigerians had never eaten or even seen noodles; many thought they were being sold worms. Yet the new offering immediately found a big market. Indomie noodles can be cooked in less than three minutes and combined with an egg to produce a nutritious, low-cost meal. The company soon shifted from importing to manufacturing the product locally. As Deepak Singhal, the CEO of Dufil Prima Foods, told us: "We created a food that was relevant for Nigeria. And in ten to fifteen years, we became a household name."

Across the continent in Kenya, there is a company with an equally impressive growth story, one also built on a fundamental innovation. Equity Bank was born out of a small building society in 2004, with just over 400,000 clients at the time. Today it has more than 12 million clients across East Africa. In 2017, it had over $5 billion in assets and reported pretax profits of $270 million.[3]

James Mwangi, Equity Bank's founding CEO, told us that Equity Bank's purpose is "to solve a social problem: lack of access to financial services." That problem was deeply personal for Mwangi: "I grew up in a rural area, and my own mother didn't have a bank account," he said. "The nearest bank branch was fifty kilometers away, and the minimum opening balance was equivalent to several years of her earnings. My mother would also have been intimidated by banks, with their granite floors, long queues, and formally dressed officials." To make matters worse, banks often had a seven-day rule between withdrawals. "If your child got sick, you couldn't go back and withdraw money from your account if you'd been there the day before," said Mwangi. "Banks simply didn't understand the financial diaries of ordinary people."

Kenyans' logical response was to keep their money under the mattress—fewer than one in ten adults had a bank account at the turn of the twenty-first century. Today, thanks in large measure to Equity Bank's innovations, two-thirds of them do. "We knew we had to address the needs of people like my mother," Mwangi said. "We wanted to give banking a human face and create the concept of the bank as a marketplace where people would feel at home. We did away with high minimum balances, created affordable products, and most importantly, delivered them where people lived." Well before cell phone–based banking came along, Equity Bank introduced what it called "mobile banking." It created mini bank branches that could fit in the back of a Land Rover and drove them from village to village across rural Kenya. Equity Bank's best-known innovation, though, is its agency banking model; it has accredited more than thirty thousand small retail outlets across the country as bank agents, able to accept deposits and dispense cash. "That has really taken banking to the last mile in every village," Mwangi told us.

Today Equity Bank has moved beyond Land Rovers and enabled true mobile banking via its Equitel cell phone banking application, launched in 2015. By 2017, Equitel was handling the large majority of the bank's cash transactions and loan disbursements, and the bank was adding insurance and brokerage service to the platform. Equity Bank is already looking at future innovations. "We see social media as the next channel for banking," said Mwangi. "So our next big focus is channel innovation."

In chapter 1, we emphasized that, to win in Africa, companies must make bold strategic moves to seize the growth opportunity in consumer and business markets, differentiate themselves from the competition, and achieve breakthrough productivity. The Indomie and Equity Bank stories provide great illustrations of those moves. Both have driven constant, systematic innovation to meet the unmet needs of African consumers and businesses. Their experience, and that of other fast-growing businesses across the continent, points to four key innovation practices that you should put at the heart of your strategy:

1. Create products and services that fulfill Africa's unmet needs.

2. Rethink your business model to truly engage with your customers.

3. Get lean to drive down cost and price points.

4. Harness technology to unleash the next wave of innovation.

INNOVATION PRACTICE 1: CREATE PRODUCTS AND SERVICES THAT FULFILL AFRICA'S UNMET NEEDS

A hallmark of innovators such as Tolaram and Equity Bank is to create new products and services—and sometimes whole categories—that are targeted at African needs, tastes, and spending power. Our survey of business executives suggests that success in this arena is a key differentiator of company performance in Africa. Among companies reporting rapid growth and high levels of profitability, 44 percent of respondents said the main focus of their growth strategy in Africa was to launch new products or services or adapt existing products to African customers' needs and preferences. Among other companies, fewer than 30 percent were doing the same.

Indomie noodles was a classic innovation to meet an unmet need that consumers struggled to satisfy. But Tolaram did not stop there: it is now seeking new opportunities to fulfill unmet needs across Africa. One such innovation—creating a packaged version of a traditional West African deep-fried snack called "chin chin"—stems from Africa's rapid urbanization and youthful demographics. "Chin chin is a household product that people used to cook at home," says CEO Singhal. "But these days, young people in the cities are relying on their grandparents to send it from the countryside. So we created a similar taste in a packaged form. We've localized and customized our product to make it relevant to the market." Indomie noodles, too, have been localized and Africanized: Tolaram took its original Asian noodle product and added local spices to appeal to West African palates.

There are many other areas where business innovators are finding solutions to Africa's unmet needs. Building affordable housing, a critical challenge in the continent's fast-growing cities, is one. LafargeHolcim, a global cement company with operations across Africa, has developed a new process that allows homebuilders to create bricks made largely of earth. The company says this reduces the cost of building a house by 20 to 40 percent. The company offers customers training, equipment to make the bricks, and designs for basic houses. LafargeHolcim's innovation is aimed squarely at making its cement products affordable to low-income customers, but it is also part of a broader social commitment. The company has helped create the Affordable Housing Hub in partnership with UN-Habitat and several international development agencies. This initiative is pioneering homebuilding and financing innovations in countries ranging from Ghana to Mali to Morocco.[4]

Africa might have an unmet need for basic bricks made of earth—but it has an equally pressing need for a wide range of high-tech gadgets such as smartphones. Chinese mobile-phone maker Tecno packs advanced technology into smartphones that retail for less than $50 and have been tailored for African customers, including photo software designed to better capture darker skin tones. In Ethiopia, it was the first major cell phone brand to introduce a keyboard in Amharic, the country's official language. Tecno is prospering in Africa, winning a market share of between 25 and 40 percent in several East African markets, despite competition from global technology leaders. As it does so, Tecno is hastening the spread of smartphone technology.[5]

One growing need in Africa is for smartcards, such as those used by Mastercard and Visa for their secure, chip-and-pin enabled credit and debit cards. Kofo Akinkugbe, a Nigeria-based former banker, spotted a gap in the market: the fact that, despite the rapidly rising penetration of banking, sub-Saharan Africa lacked an internationally certified manufacturer of smartcards. In response, she launched SecureID in 2005. "I saw a very large white space," Akinkugbe told us, "Banks were issuing cards in increasing numbers, but the ecosystem was driven by importers of cards who did not project the global best practices the banks expected."

SecureID overcame multiple hurdles to build a state-of-the-art smartcard manufacturing plant near Lagos. Not the least of these was convincing global card issuers that they could trust her. "The challenge was to get certified by Mastercard, Visa, and American Express, given Nigeria's reputation for fraud," Akinkugbe said. So SecureID invested in building a plant that conformed to the highest international specifications— including biometric access control, closed-circuit TV, cyber-security tested by the firm's own team of hackers, a water treatment plant to supply the plant's sophisticated machinery, and equipment to eliminate dust from the manufacturing environment. When we visited the shining, windowless facility, we could have been in Dallas or Frankfurt—but for the nationality of the smartly uniformed workers, 95 percent of whom are Nigerian. The card issuers were equally impressed: they certified the plant within six months.

Today SecureID issues more than 30 million smartcards a year and counts many global and local banks as its clients. Akinkugbe sees plenty more unmet needs to address. SecureID is already supplying SIM cards to mobile phone companies and has expanded its manufacturing capacity to supply secure passports, ID cards, and driver's licenses, which have historically been produced outside of Africa, at great expense to public-sector agencies and inconvenience to citizens. Said Akinkugbe, "The Nigerian newspapers were full of articles saying, 'I applied for my driver's license and I still haven't got it after two years.' But when the government commissioned us to make license cards in our local plant, we could get them into the hands of the driver in a week or two—and save the country a lot of foreign exchange."

INNOVATION PRACTICE 2: RETHINK YOUR BUSINESS MODEL TO TRULY ENGAGE YOUR CUSTOMERS

Equity Bank's innovation of turning thousands of shopkeepers into banking agents was a brilliant move to solve the problem of last-mile delivery. That is a challenge for businesses in almost any sector: Africa is a vast continent with generally poor transport infrastructure and big gaps in communications. Many millions of people lack formal postal addresses, or even a street name. While English or French may be the common tongue in the big cities, many rural people speak only their local language—of which there are more than 1,000 across the continent. Nigeria alone has more than 500 languages, Cameroon has 250, and Kenya has 68.

When we met with James Mwangi, he reflected on how his team had shaped the agency banking model: "We asked, how can we use shopkeepers as outlets to serve our customers? It took us six years to convince the Central Bank that shopkeepers could accept cash as banking agents. But once we did, we were able to multiply our network a thousandfold." As a result, he added, "banking now competes with sugar and salt as a product." The agency model has also demystified banking. Mwangi says: "Our agents don't talk to customers in banking jargon—they use the language of the common man." The agents have benefited too. As Mwangi notes, "We've helped those thirty thousand shopkeepers professionalize. They've become owner-managers, managing a bank for a commission. That in turn has distributed wealth across the country."

Margaret Wanjiku, who runs a pharmacy in a suburb of Nairobi, is one of Equity Bank's many agents. She told us that she typically serves between twenty and fifty Equity Bank customers each day, who mostly make cash withdrawals and deposits.

"Around month end, there might be one hundred customers coming in over a couple of days," she said. That traffic has helped her grow the pharmacy business, too. Customers appreciate the convenience of the agency model. "Equity Bank agencies are just all over, so you can drop in anywhere," said one customer at Wanjiku's pharmacy. "It's really made my business faster and safer," said another, who runs an informal trading stall. "I don't have to carry a lot of money from one place to another, because there's an agent just next to where I work."

Tolaram, too, has driven fundamental innovation in getting Indomie noodles to consumers throughout Nigeria, starting with its approach to marketing. The company created a TV and radio ad campaign targeted at children. One ad features a young girl skipping down a supermarket aisle to grab handfuls of Indomie noodles packets as her mother, following with the shopping cart, smiles approvingly. "Changing people's eating habits is not easy," Deepak Singhal told us. "So we decided to start with the children and go all the way up." Indomie's fan club is a key part of this marketing campaign: it has branches in more than three thousand primary schools, which it supports with activities such as art competitions and excursions for pupils and teachers.

Tolaram supports its highly visible brand with a vast "feet-on-the-street" distribution network that includes more than a thousand vehicles, including motorcycles, trucks, and tuk-tuks (three-wheeled mini autos common throughout Africa and Asia). When distributors can't go any further by vehicle, they continue on foot. That was a critical innovation, since the company's route to consumers was through thousands of small, often informal outlets rather than an organized supermarket network. "Remember," says Singhal, "in many African countries, 90 percent of retail outlets are informal." Tolaram has also made sure that every time consumers walk into a local mom-and-pop store or stop at a stall at an open market, they find Indomie noodles right in front of them. The strategy is simple. Rather than trying to push its noodles to retailers, Tolaram focuses on getting its consumers excited about the product. They in turn ask for Indomie every time they go to their local store. That creates a tremendous pull from shopkeepers and stallholders, who beg Indomie's distributors to keep them stocked. Our local research in Nigeria suggests that some small retailers spend as much as half their working capital stocking Indomie.

Tolaram has also innovated in other aspects of its business model. "We have our own logistics company, our own raw material, our own plants, and our own packaging facilities," says Singhal. "Controlling our own supply chain is very important. The consistency and quality of supply is essential." As we discuss in chapter 5, such "backward integration" is a key step that companies can take to weather Africa's relatively high volatility and ensure their businesses are resilient to shocks. Tolaram's integrated supply chain, along with its logistics expertise and distribution network, made it the ideal partner for Kellogg as the American company sought to ramp up its presence in Africa.

PZ Cussons, a British consumer goods company with operations in Africa, has also driven real innovation to meet the challenge of getting its household goods, electrical appliances, and health and beauty products to customers. In Nigeria, it has a roster of hundreds of small distributors who serve small retailers. In some cities, it operates Coolworld stores to sell refrigerators, freezers, and other appliances. It has also set up twenty-five cash-and-carry depots in Nigeria, with a separate warehouse for each product category. Traders bring their own trucks to load up on everything from Imperial Leather soap to evaporated milk, taking on much of the company's last-mile delivery.[6] Coca-Cola, too, has set up foot and motorbike delivery systems across Africa and uses advanced analytics to predict restocking schedules at hundreds of informal kiosks.

The companies described above have all grappled with Africa's infrastructure challenges in ways that ultimately strengthen their businesses, giving them a significant advantage over competitors who have not invested the same time and money.

INNOVATION PRACTICE 3: GET LEAN TO DRIVE DOWN COST AND PRICE POINTS

Even if African incomes have grown steadily in recent years, average incomes remain low by global standards. Of course, there are also big opportunities for companies to serve business customers and government institutions, but in these markets too, affordability is often the decisive factor. To profitably serve African customers in meaningful numbers—as Indomie and Equity Bank have both done—companies need to build high efficiency and low cost into their business models. In James Mwangi's words: "Your business model needs high volumes and low margins, and it needs to be cost-effective and technology-driven." Equity Bank has lived up to that promise: it reduced its cost-to-income ratio to 49 percent in 2016, down from a high of 70 percent some years previously. (By way of comparison, the average cost-to-income ratio of all banks in McKinsey's global banking database is 59 percent.[7])

It is worth noting that Equity Bank's efficiency drive is part of a broader push by the African banking sector, which has seen its cost-to-income ratio edge downward in recent years. But we see big opportunities for banks in Africa to get leaner by applying three main levers. The first is digitization: there is a major opportunity to migrate distribution costs to digital channels such as Equity Bank's Equitel platform. That will also allow banks to automate customer journeys, such as taking out a loan, and back-office processes. The second lever is to improve frontline productivity though analytics and data. The third is to consolidate back-office functions to reduce head office costs.[8]

Indeed, the recent slowdown in economic growth in some major African economies has been a spur for efficiency in many companies. Among Africa-based respondents to our executive survey, 48 percent reported that their companies' African revenues had increased over the past five years, yet 67 percent said their profitability had improved—a clear sign of improved efficiency even in challenging operating conditions. Those that have driven down costs will emerge leaner and ready to compete more effectively when growth picks up again. An example is Ecobank in Nigeria, which launched a major efficiency drive in 2016. It closed fifty branches and reduced back-office costs through innovative approaches such as laying off drivers and partnering with Uber to retrain them as Uber drivers. The bank also appointed a new procurement team that renegotiated supplier contracts and signed on new suppliers, resulting in procurement costs being reduced by 40 to 50 percent.

One compelling reason to boost efficiency is the mounting competition that companies face in Africa, including from a new wave of Chinese-owned businesses that have embarked on an ambitious expansion drive. Consider China's StarTimes broadcasting company, which set up its first African operation in Rwanda in 2007 and within a decade was providing digital satellite television to 4 million customers in thirteen African countries and four languages. Satellite television was traditionally the preserve of higher-income households, but StarTimes targeted a broader market, pricing its subscription packages as low as $2 a month. In ten years, it has become a leading pay television provider across Africa. In Tanzania, for example, it invested $120 million over the 2010–2016 period and reduced the local cost of pay television by 80 to 90 percent.[9]

In construction and real estate, Chinese firms have won nearly 50 percent market share of Africa's international construction market. China's own breakneck pace of infrastructure construction over the past three decades has produced contractors with some of the most efficient cost structures in the world. The Chinese government's financing of African infrastructure has helped Chinese contractors win some bids, but even in open-tender projects sponsored by the World Bank, Chinese firms are the biggest winners, winning 42 percent of contracts by value. One African government official we interviewed described Chinese firms as routinely being 40 percent cheaper than the next-lowest bid for similar levels of quality.[10]

INNOVATION PRACTICE 4: HARNESS TECHNOLOGY TO UNLEASH THE NEXT WAVE OF INNOVATION

Our executive survey suggests that winning companies are moving fast to embrace digital and mobile technologies and incorporate them into their innovation strategies. Among companies reporting rapid growth and high levels of profitability, 39 percent of respondents said mobile technologies were a key element of their African growth strategies, compared with 24 percent among all other companies. Likewise, 34 percent of high performers are putting social media tools at the heart of their strategy (compared with 15 percent for other companies), while 31 percent envisage making major use of big data and analytics (24 percent for other companies). High performers are also ahead on the next generation of technology innovations: they are twice as likely as other companies to put the internet of things and blockchain at the heart of their strategy for the next five years (figure 4-1).

FIGURE 4-1

High-performing firms put technology at the heart of their Africa growth strategy

Question: Which technologies will most support your organization's growth in Africa in the next five years?[1] % of respondents

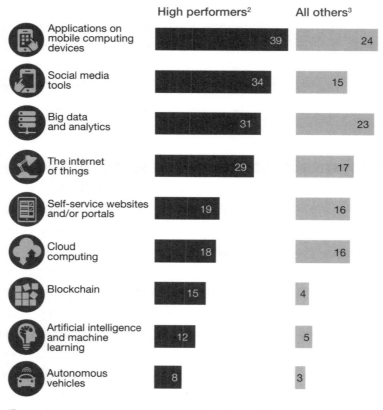

	High performers[2]	All others[3]
Applications on mobile computing devices	39	24
Social media tools	34	15
Big data and analytics	31	23
The internet of things	29	17
Self-service websites and/or portals	19	16
Cloud computing	18	16
Blockchain	15	4
Artificial intelligence and machine learning	12	5
Autonomous vehicles	8	3

[1]Respondents who answered "other" or "don't know" are not shown.
[2]Respondents in high-performing companies, n = 166.
[3]Respondents in all other companies n = 603.
Source: McKinsey Insights executive survey on business in Africa, 2017.

We were not surprised that the respondents in our executive survey saw digital and mobile technologies as the single biggest business opportunity in Africa. Even in parts of Africa where internet access is still patchy or nonexistent, digital technology is changing the landscape. Thanks to companies like Interswitch, electronic payments are sweeping across the region. There are already 100 million active users of mobile financial services, and this number could multiply if the rest of the continent follows the lead of Kenya, where virtually every adult holds a mobile money account. That penetration is thanks to the explosive growth of M-Pesa, the service that led the way in mobile money in Africa. Launched by mobile telecommunications operator Safaricom in 2007, today it provides cell phone–based banking services to tens of millions of people.[11]

LIGHTBULB MOMENT: INNOVATIONS IN OFF-GRID ENERGY

The widespread use of mobile money in Africa represents a big opportunity for entrepreneurs—and some of the most innovative have harnessed services such as M-Pesa to bring solar-powered energy to African households. The largest player in this fast-growing sector is Kenya-based M-Kopa. Founded with venture capital backing in 2011, the company provides affordable solar-powered electricity generation and storage solutions to households—and finances repayment over a twelve-month period via mobile money accounts. By 2017, M-Kopa had sold more than six hundred thousand household kits—double the number of the previous year. Most of its sales to date have been in Kenya, but the company has also established businesses in Tanzania, Uganda, and Ghana. In a sign of global business interest in Africa's off-grid energy movement, the Japanese conglomerate Mitsui acquired a stake in M-Kopa in 2018.

Several other off-grid energy startups are growing fast in Africa, making the sector both increasingly competitive and an arena for continued innovation. One example is Uganda-based Fenix, which by 2017 had sold one hundred and forty thousand of its solar-power kits, also enabled by mobile money, to African households. In late 2017, Fenix was acquired by ENGIE, a major global energy company based in France, which announced plans to reach millions more off-grid solar-power customers across Africa and beyond. Another startup is UK-based BBOXX, which distributes its solar kits through agents in ten African countries—and uses remote monitoring technology to improve battery life and users' experience. Yet another firm is d.light, which focuses on selling affordable solar-powered appliances such as a $12 rechargeable lantern.

Let's take a closer look at M-Kopa, whose CEO is Canadian-born Jesse Moore. The name his cofounders chose for the business provides a clue to their original idea: *kopa* means "borrow" in Swahili, not "electricity." M-Kopa planned to harness the mobile-money revolution unleashed by M-Pesa to enable Africans to finance the purchase of appliances that had hitherto been out of their reach, such as televisions and refrigerators. "Our idea was to create the 'electronic sachet,'" said Moore. "Just as companies like Unilever sell shampoo in sachets to make it affordable to lower-income households, we would use mobile money to apply the same principle to selling appliances." Using their M-Pesa account, a Kenyan household would be able to pay off its first refrigerator in monthly installments. Almost immediately, though, the company came up against a barrier: without electric power, no one would buy a fridge or a TV. And so the business idea morphed to being about loans *and* power: the first thing M-Kopa would offer via mobile-money financing would be a solar-power kit. That, in turn, would open the market for appliances and provide the company with a loyal customer base that had already proven its willingness and ability to make regular monthly payments.

Even with mobile-enabled installment payments, there was a big question about whether ordinary African households had the disposable income to afford solar energy kits—let alone fridges and TVs. Around 70 percent of African households earn less than $5,000 a year, and only a small number are middle-class by Western standards. But the M-Kopa business model takes that obstacle into account. As Moore told us, "Ours is a displacement proposition. African households already spend a lot of money on crappy energy sources like kerosene and batteries. We enable them to stop that wasteful expenditure and switch to something cheaper and better. It turns out that solar energy is a secret freer of cash, which people can reapply to buy fridges or pay school fees."

M-Kopa is making real progress against its original, seemingly quixotic objective of selling appliances to rural African households. "We've created a financial relationship with our customers," said Moore. "Once they've paid off their solar kit, we can sell them something else." By the end of 2017, nearly two hundred thousand customers had returned for a second M-Kopa purchase, ranging from a larger solar kit to a refrigerator to a fuel-efficient stove. The best-seller, though, is an LED television that M-Kopa has developed to operate off solar power: as of 2017, the company had sold one hundred thousand of them. "We've helped people move from kerosene to content!" says Moore.

Although M-Kopa had yet to turn a profit at the time of writing, its revenues have grown rapidly and it has had no trouble in attracting multiple rounds of investment from global investors betting on its long-term success. "We're already making $1 million a week in revenues, and will soon hit $100 million a year," Moore told us in late 2017. "We plan to achieve profitability within quarters rather than years." The company is prioritizing long-term growth and is actively investing in opportunities that could turn out to be big revenue streams in future. One of those is data. M-Kopa assiduously collects information on its customers' spending patterns and preferences. And so M-Kopa is tackling yet another of Africa's business barriers—the scarcity of reliable consumer data. "In the long run, data might prove to be the most powerful tool in our treasure chest," Moore told us.

If you take a drive around rural Kenya, you'll see off-grid energy changing lives, one homestead at a time. One of them, in the foothills of Mount Kilimanjaro in Kenya's Kajiado County, belongs to Duncan Manga and his family. Lacking a connection to the grid, Manga signed up with M-Kopa in 2015. When we visited him, he told us that electricity had changed his family's life. "My children can study at night, we can light up our kitchen, and I can charge my phone—before, I had to take it somewhere else to charge," he said. "It's also improved our security. Before, hyenas would come at night and attack our goats; now they see the lights and are scared off. Our lives have gotten much better. We used to travel far to buy kerosene for our lamp, and when it ran out, we were in darkness. Now we have light."

TECHNOLOGY FOR TRANSFORMATION

Equity Bank, too, is using technology-driven innovation to support its goal of becoming ever more efficient in serving its customers. Its Equitel mobile application uses SIM overlay technology to enable easy access by customers of every mobile provider. The value of transactions completed via Equitel exceeded $3.5 billion in 2016, up from $1 billion in 2015. "It's become very big, very fast," Mwangi told us. "Today, our branches are doing 5,000 transactions a day, our agents are doing 300,000 transactions a day, and Equitel is doing 900,000 transactions a day. So we're really moving away from bricks and mortar. And it's also moved our bank to a variable-cost model." As the proportion of transactions undertaken and loans dispersed in branches has fallen, Equity has begun to shrink its branch network.

Many more entrepreneurs are seizing the space being opened up by rising technology penetration. In Nigeria, Stanford-educated Tayo Oviosu founded Paga in 2009 as a mobile money transfer service in response to his frustration with having to carry cash. Customers can use Paga to send money to anyone in Nigeria either from their mobile phone or internet-enabled device or via any Paga agent across the country. Recipients get the money instantly, without having to be registered Paga users. Customers can also use Paga to pay for a variety of goods and services such as electricity bills, cable TV subscriptions, and prepaid mobile airtime top-ups. By April 2018, it had signed up over 8.4 million users and was processing close to $2 billion a year in payments. Even in the tough market conditions in Nigeria following the 2016 oil price collapse, Paga kept growing fast. Oviosu told us: "We are still achieving 166 percent growth, year on year. We doubled our revenues in the first quarter of 2018 compared to the same quarter in the previous year. In fact, we are showing people greater value using the Paga wallet in this tough economic climate."

Companies that harness digital technologies for innovation can also help usher in transformative change in other sectors that are crucial in strengthening African economies and societies, including education and health care.

In education, consider the example of the African Leadership University (ALU), which operates in Rwanda and Mauritius.

It offers a blended program that mixes online education with peer-to-peer learning and in-person interaction with faculty. Its founder, Fred Swaniker, told us, "Our university produces talent that competes with students from Harvard and Stanford. But we do it using one-tenth of their real estate and at one-tenth to one-twentieth of their cost." His innovation was to shape a business model for higher education from scratch. Universities were invented "in a world where information was scarce," he said. "But today, we live in a world where knowledge is ubiquitous." Rather than relying on the traditional, professor-centered learning model, the ALU took a multimodal approach where individual students manage their own education using technology, peer-to-peer learning with classmates, and four-month work-experience internships with partner companies. That enables the university to get by with a small team of teaching staff.

In 2017, US-based educational technology company 2U ponied up $103 million to acquire a South African startup called GetSmarter. Founded in 2008 by brothers Sam and Rob Paddock, GetSmarter offers online certification courses to distance-learning students in partnership with several of the world's top-tier universities. It has served more than fifty thousand students globally with a course-completion rate averaging 90 percent. The company says it earned approximately $17 million in revenue in 2016 and has some four hundred employees, including performance coaches, technologists, and video producers, as well as academic tutors who operate remotely around the world.[12]

In health care, digital technologies are enabling greater use of remote diagnosis, treatment, and education. Again, there are exciting opportunities for digital startups to contribute to these outcomes while building profitable businesses. One example is the mPedigree Network, which offers a technology-based solution to combat the sale of counterfeit products. Using mPedigree's software, manufacturers can label their product packaging with a random code hidden beneath a scratch-off covering. To authenticate a product, the consumer simply scratches off the covering and sends the code via mobile phone to a toll-free number. mPedigree has been particularly successful in protecting pharmaceutical companies and their consumers from counterfeit drugs—a pressing need in Africa, given the preponderance of informal distribution and retail channels.[13]

Equity Bank, too, is innovating in the health-care space— both to contribute to society and to build a business in a new sector. Its innovation was to launch a network of medical centers called Equity Afia, linked to a health insurance product offered by the bank. The inspiration came from its charitable foundation, which has awarded some fifteen thousand university scholarships to gifted students from across Kenya's forty-seven counties. "We looked at our graduates and found that six hundred of them had been to medical school," said James Mwangi. Equity Bank already knew that 40 percent of the defaults on its bank loans were due to ill health in the family. "So we empowered our medical graduates as entrepreneur doctors, helping them start clinics and giving them the IT system backbone," said Mwangi. "At the same time, we are providing our customers with medical insurance. These products intertwine the commercial interests of the bank and a solution to address the health challenge of our society." In early 2018, Equity Afia had five medical centers up and running; Mwangi's vision is to help three hundred doctors open clinics across Kenya.[14]

Equity Bank's expansion into health care, incidentally, points to a key strategic approach of many of the continent's most ambitious businesses. In our executive survey,

25 percent of top-performing companies in Africa said their growth strategies included entering adjacent industry sectors or expanding into new customer segments; just 11 percent of other companies planned to do the same.

───────────

To turn white space into gold—for shareholders and customers alike—companies must be ready to rethink their products, services, markets, and business models. For forward-looking businesses, that makes Africa one of the world's most exciting arenas for innovation. Companies like Tolaram, Equity Bank, and M-Kopa provide examples that can be an inspiration to others: they have found ways to overcome persistent challenges that limited markets, hampered business growth, and made life harder for ordinary people. The innovative solutions that make business growth possible in Africa could one day provide more efficient products, services and business models for the rest of the world.

CHAPTER 5

BUILD RESILIENCE FOR THE LONG TERM

In the first part of this book, we highlighted the extraordinary growth potential of Africa's manufacturing sector, which could double in value to nearly $1 trillion by 2025, driven largely by meeting the continent's own demand. But, as noted, industrialists will need to overcome many barriers if they are to realize that potential—getting access to suitable land and sufficient capital, ensuring sufficient power supply, and complying with local regulations that can often be complex and unpredictable.

Aliko Dangote, arguably Africa's most successful industrialist, is acutely aware of these barriers—and has built workarounds into his strategy, even as he has watched competitors trip up and go out of business. Dangote started business as a trader of cement, rice, and sugar in 1978. In the 1990s, he spotted an opportunity to substitute some of the products he was importing by manufacturing them himself. "As a trading company, we had the infrastructure, the logistics, the warehouses, the customers," he told us. "But we were importing the goods we sold; for example, pasta from Italy. So we decided the only way forward for us was industrialization."

Dangote has since built thriving businesses producing not just pasta but also sugar, salt, flour, plastics, and cement. His cement company has grown to become West Africa's largest listed company, with sixteen thousand employees and operations in Nigeria and nine other countries—Cameroon, Ghana, Ethiopia, Congo, Senegal, Sierra Leone, South Africa, Tanzania, and Zambia. He hasn't stopped there: in 2015, his company began building a 650,000-barrel-a-day petroleum refinery near Lagos. In 2016, the company broke ground on a massive fertilizer plant next door, planned to be Africa's largest. To supply these facilities, Dangote is also constructing an almost seven-hundred-mile gas pipeline from Nigeria's oil region.

Yet the company's decision to build manufacturing businesses was taken with full awareness of the risks. Dangote said, "We knew that everyone who had tried industrialization in Nigeria pre-1995 had gone out of business. So we took a deep look at the impediments, and we realized that there were two major problems that were making manufacturers fail. First, there was no reliable electric power. Second, there were major inconsistencies in government policies." To mitigate these risks, the Dangote Group determined that it would generate its own power and build close relationships with government. "We would just keep making them understand that constant policy change does not work," Dangote told us.

Because the barriers to business in Africa can be so daunting, even well-established local firms like Dangote have had to work hard to build resilience into their business models.

As global multinationals and foreign investors grow their footprint in Africa, they need to do the same. When we examined the tactics of the Dangote Group and other companies that have successfully managed Africa's risks and uncertainties, we identified four essential practices. If your business is going to be sturdy enough to withstand the sandstorms of the Sahara and the thunderstorms of Southern Africa, it will have to be built on these cornerstones:

1. Take a long-term view and ride out short-term volatility.

2. Diversify by building a balanced portfolio across countries or sectors.

3. Integrate up and down your value chain.

4. Understand local context and claim a place at the table with governments.

CORNERSTONE 1: TAKE A LONG-TERM VIEW— AND RIDE OUT SHORT-TERM VOLATILITY

Aliko Dangote thought long and hard before he took the plunge and invested his money in building factories in Africa. That process of investigation led him to spend several months in Brazil—another big emerging market where industrialists faced tough operating conditions. "I did a lot of research, spent time in factories, and really thought through the challenges," he told us. "At the time, Brazilian manufacturers were dealing with hyperinflation and massive exchange-rate problems."

Dangote returned to Nigeria with a clear insight: to succeed as an industrialist, he would need to take a bold, long-term approach: "I realized that if we were going to build industries in Africa, we would have to be the boldest people around. If we weren't going to be bold, we could just forget it." Just as important, he recognized that he would need to be ready to fight for his business if necessary. "I didn't start my manufacturing businesses assuming I'd have zero problems. I'd said, 'Even if there are problems, I'll solve them.'" Dangote soon had opportunities to put these lessons into action. For example, he was offered a 30 percent stake in a new sugar-refinery project in Nigeria—only to see his partner pull out when costs began to mount. Dangote not only decided to go forward on his own, he increased the plant's capacity by another 50 percent.

Dangote has no doubt that foreign-owned businesses can do well in Africa—but only if they are willing to make equally bold commitments and view the continent as a long-term play. "You don't have to be African to succeed in Africa," he says. "But if you really want to do business here, you have to think long-term. Africa is not a place where you can come and invest for two or three years, milk the business, and run away. You have to build a business that can succeed in the good times, the okay times, and the bad times."

His views are echoed by several of the African leaders we spoke to when writing this book. Ngozi Okonjo-Iweala, former minister of finance of Nigeria, said: "The most successful businesses are ones that take the long view. There are real risks, although I think they're exaggerated. But long-term opportunities are abundant, and the returns are significant. So businesses must come in willing to be in it for the long term—and be willing to take the risk and look at the real fundamentals."

Ashish J. Thakkar is a British-Ugandan entrepreneur who founded Mara Corporation, which has technology, real estate, and financial services businesses spanning twenty-five African countries. He also cofounded the Atlas Mara financial services group with former Barclays CEO Bob Diamond. Thakkar told us: "I don't think you should come to our continent unless you have a long-term lens." Companies that take the long view realize that, even if Africa's economic volatility can make operating conditions tough, it also presents "phenomenal opportunities."

Thakkar draws an analogy between Africa today and the United States at the turn of the twentieth century. "Think about how the United States was built by the big investors in the late 1800s and early 1900s. None of them were short term—they stayed and reinvested in their country. We need to look at Africa in a similar fashion and mobilize long-term, scalable, sustainable capital that is going to really stay with us." That, he said, will be a win-win for businesses and the economies they invest in.

The high-performing companies in our executive survey agree: fully half of them say that a long-term view is one of their most important strategies for managing the economic and political risks of operating in Africa. Average performers are much less likely to adopt this posture. The survey findings also contain a warning that some Western businesses may be taking a short-term approach that will do them no favors in Africa. Just 31 percent of North American respondents, for example, said their companies viewed Africa as a long-term investment. African-based respondents were twice as likely to focus on the long term. The danger for those taking a next-quarter view of Africa is that the bumps along the road might knock them out of the game altogether—leaving the continent's growth opportunities to others, like Dangote, that have a longer horizon.

Western firms that balk at making a long-term commitment in Africa could also put themselves at a disadvantage against another key competitor: Chinese industrialists. Foreign direct investment from China increased at a breakneck annual growth rate of 40 percent between 2005 and 2015.[1] In a McKinsey survey of over one thousand Chinese-owned companies operating in Africa's major economies, nearly half of them reported that they had made capital-intensive investments—for example, building factories or purchasing manufacturing equipment. Given that most Chinese firms are relatively new entrants in Africa, that signals a strong long-term commitment.

Our own analysis bears out the importance of taking a long view. Companies that have made long-term investments and shaped strategies with a decades-long outlook have generally outperformed their competitors. That holds true globally: for example, McKinsey research found that US companies that adopted a long-term approach earned revenues 47 percent higher than their short-term-focused peers between 2001 and 2014. They invested more, and more consistently, than other companies; they were more interested in sustainable revenue and earnings growth than in meeting short-term targets; and they created thousands more jobs.[2] We believe that these practices are even more important in Africa, where a longer-term commitment can enable companies to see past near-term volatility to build robust brands, supply chains, distribution networks, and relationships with governments and other stakeholders.

A short-term approach, on the other hand, can do real damage to your brand and reputation. One global technology firm, for example, pulled out of Nigeria when that country was undergoing a bout of macroeconomic volatility. The problem was, the company left its clients high and dry; for example, a bank that had bought expensive equipment from the tech firm was unable to get it serviced. Years later, the company returned to Nigeria to find its reputation still damaged—its business customers had long memories. In a volatile environment, customers value brands that give them certainty and reliability.

CORNERSTONE 2: DIVERSIFY YOUR AFRICAN PORTFOLIO

To build resilience to the operational challenges of manufacturing in Africa, the Dangote Group deliberately diversified across industries and geographies. "There's no sector that's permanently healthy," Aliko Dangote says. "If today cement is excellent in Nigeria, it might not be in the next five years. So we're fully diversified across different products, as well as downstream, midstream, and upstream."

Brewer SABMiller also adopted a strategy of geographic diversification as a deliberate move to build long-term resilience into its billion-dollar African business. "We ended up with a portfolio of medium-sized businesses in forty-four countries," said Mark Bowman, the company's former Africa head. "None of our bets was very big. And our portfolio would self-compensate. So if something went wrong in Angola with the currency, for example, it would be offset by an overperformance in Nigeria and Tanzania. The overall construction of the portfolio was a very smart tool in ensuring that our business in Africa did well. There were too many variables to get everything working perfectly every time. We knew that on balance, though, the portfolio would perform."

If you are a large business in Africa, like Dangote, it also makes sense to add non-African countries to your portfolio: the company's diversification across multiple African countries could soon be followed by diversification into other regions. Dangote has announced plans to invest $20 billion–$50 billion in the United States and Europe between 2020 and 2025, in industries including renewable energy and petrochemicals.

Again, the findings of our executive survey support such diversification strategies. Nearly half of high-performing companies in the survey reported that they were diversified across countries, sectors or both. Only around a third of lower-performing companies reported the same.

To delve deeper into the benefits of diversification, we analyzed several consumer goods companies in Africa. Our aim was to understand how the volatility of their profits over a five-year period correlated with the number of countries they operate in. The findings were unequivocal: the returns of companies operating in only one country were more than twice as volatile as those of firms exposed to multiple markets. We conducted the same exercise for banks, and found that those with branches in two to five countries experienced much lower volatility in their 2012–2015 profits than those operating in a single country.

However, there are also risks in expanding into too many countries too fast. Our analysis found that banks operating in six or more African countries actually experienced greater volatility in profits than their midsized peers. Indeed, several firms operating in the financial services sector told us they were being cautious about expanding their geographic portfolios too fast, to avoid taking on too much complexity. M-Kopa, the Kenya-based solar power and financing startup, has already expanded into Ghana, Tanzania, and Uganda—but its CEO, Jesse Moore, told us the company was being careful in expanding further. "We'll be in a dozen countries in due course," he said, "but I really believe some startups are expanding across borders too quickly. When you enter a new market, perhaps particularly so in Africa, you take on a lot of complexity and must navigate different legal frameworks, tax laws, and cultures." For M-Kopa, like Paga (see chapter 4), the focus is on growing the number of customers it serves—not the number of countries it operates in. "We're only at 10 percent penetration in Kenya," said Moore. "We have much more growth ahead of us in the markets we're already in."

Our executive survey confirms the importance of constructing your geographic portfolio to achieve the twin goals of increasing diversification *and* limiting complexity. Around a third of all respondents said that operating only in African markets they know well was a key strategy for avoiding undue complexity and managing political and economic risk. African-based companies were even more likely to adopt this approach. International firms can take a leaf out of their book: don't underestimate the risks involved in entering a new market, and plan your geographic expansion step by step.

One tool designed to help investors balance their portfolios is McKinsey's African Stability Index, which we designed to support businesses and investors to balance their portfolios— and help policymakers to understand and then address their country's vulnerabilities. The index measures three stability factors that have equal weighting. The first is the country's macroeconomic stability, which reflects its gross debt-to-GDP ratio and its external balances measured by reserves in months of imports. The second is its economic diversification measured by resources as a share of exports. The third is social and political stability, which includes unemployment levels, the Ibrahim Index of African Governance, and the number of incidents of violence as measured by the Uppsala Conflict Data Program. Each country's stability ranking is then plotted against its compound annual GDP growth rate between 2012 and 2017 (figure 5-1).[3] We regularly update the analysis and have observed significant shifts in the positions of some countries since we first published the African Stability Index in 2016.

FIGURE 5-1

McKinsey's African Stability Index pinpoints countries' growth and risk profiles[1]

Comparison of historical GDP growth rates to country stability rankings[2]

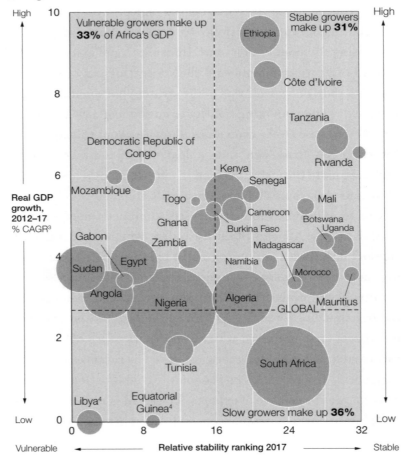

[1]The index covers 30 economies accounting for 97% of Africa's GDP.
[2]Bubble size represents country GDP estimate, 2016.
[3]Compound annual growth rate.
[4]Equatorial Guinea and Libya are plotted manually because of negative growth rates over this period.

Source: McKinsey Global Institute analysis.

Three distinct groups of countries emerge from this analysis, each accounting for around a third of Africa's GDP:

- **STABLE GROWERS:** The many countries in this group include Côte d'Ivoire, Ethiopia, Kenya, Morocco, Rwanda, Senegal, and Tanzania. These economies are relatively less dependent on resources for growth and are progressing with economic reforms and increasing their competitiveness.

- **VULNERABLE GROWERS:** These countries each have at least one of three types of vulnerability. Some, such as Angola, Nigeria, and Zambia, are heavily dependent on resource exports. For example, the 2014 fall in the oil price prompted a major growth slowdown in Angola and Nigeria from which they are only now recovering. Other countries, such as the DRC, face security or governance challenges. Finally, countries such as Mozambique are vulnerable to macroeconomic difficulties. For investors, vulnerable growers still offer promising growth potential, but they also pose risks that need to be properly assessed and understood.

- **SLOW GROWERS:** This group includes Libya and Tunisia, countries affected by the Arab Spring (although Egypt's economic recovery has lifted it out of the slow-grower group). Perhaps surprisingly to non-African investors, this group also includes Africa's second-largest economy, South Africa. Given that country's scale, investors will need to assess growth opportunities at the sector level or use their activities in this slow grower as a base from which to expand into other parts of the region.

As this analysis suggests, your Africa strategy should be built on a close understanding of the distinct risk profiles and growth trajectories of the continent's fifty-four economies. A one-size-fits-all approach is no more likely to succeed in Africa than it is in Asia or Europe. As Tidjane Thiam, CEO of Credit Suisse, says: "In any continent, different countries present different risks." In Thiam's view, many global investors miss that point and regard Africa as an exotic place where volatility and instability are constant and systemic. "I often wish people were more rational about Africa," he told us. "Its diversity and its challenges have much in common with other emerging markets. Africa is not a special continent on another planet."

CORNERSTONE 3: INTEGRATE UP AND DOWN YOUR VALUE CHAIN

In addition to diversifying across sectors and countries, the Dangote Group has also diversified up and down the supply chain, and in the process has built a highly integrated business that is resilient to shocks in its supply chain. The company's push for backward integration involves producing its own raw materials on a massive scale: in 2017 the group announced that it would invest $4.6 billion over the next three years in sugar, rice, and dairy production alone. That will eliminate the company's reliance on imported materials and the foreign exchange headaches that come with it. Aliko Dangote's vision extends beyond his own company, though: his aim is to help make Nigeria self-sufficient in food production. "When you look at it—not just in Nigeria but in the rest of Africa—the majority of countries here depend on imported food," he says. "Nigeria alone imports 4.8 million tons of wheat a year. We have land, we have water, we have the climate. We shouldn't be a massive importer of food."

Our executive survey suggests that high-performing companies in Africa are twice as likely as other firms to integrate their supply chains. Among the fast-growing, highly profitable companies in our sample, 31 percent said they had vertically integrated their supply chains to ensure reliable access to inputs. Only 16 percent of lower-performing companies had done the same (figure 5-2). That suggests that building a robust

FIGURE 5-2

High-performing companies actively manage the challenges of doing business in Africa

Our Africa business survey shows back-up power, distribution, and supply chain are top priorities.

What practices does your organization follow to overcome some of the barriers to doing business in Africa?[1] % of respondents

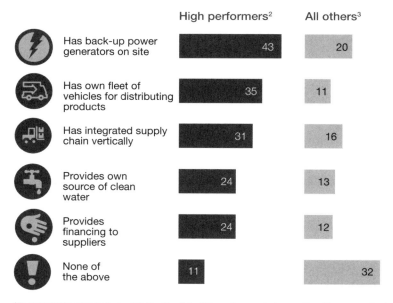

	High performers[2]	All others[3]
Has back-up power generators on site	43	20
Has own fleet of vehicles for distributing products	35	11
Has integrated supply chain vertically	31	16
Provides own source of clean water	24	13
Provides financing to suppliers	24	12
None of the above	11	32

[1]Respondents who answered "other" or "don't know" are not shown. Question was asked only of those who said they have been to at least one country in Africa, that 5% or more of their organizations' current revenue is earned in Africa, and that their organizations operate in at least one African country.
[2]Respondents in high-performing companies, n = 164.
[3]Respondents in all other companies n = 589.

Source: McKinsey Insights executive survey on business in Africa, 2017.

ecosystem of partners, as discussed in chapter 3, is a necessary step to succeed in Africa, but not the whole answer. Companies should also be ready to integrate what would usually be outsourced; otherwise, insufficiently developed supply chains or incomplete distribution networks could hamper your growth.

One such vertically integrated business is Zambeef, the Zambian meat supplier featured in chapter 2. It owns every step of the supply chain, from pasture to supermarket meat counter. Another is Tanzania-based MeTL, a conglomerate making everything from bicycles to soft drinks to textiles. MeTL operates across the agricultural value chain; it has sisal farms, tea estates, and cashew farms and a warehousing and distribution operation. The company's vertical integration is most visible in its textile business, which starts with cotton farms and continues through manufacturing finished garments. In effect, MeTL has become its own supplier of everything from raw inputs to power and water. It has also expanded into financial services, real estate, energy, and petroleum and has announced goals of reaching $5 billion in revenues by 2020, mostly by expanding into Mozambique, Malawi, Uganda, Burundi, Zambia, and Rwanda.[4] (As we discuss below, MeTL's growth has also been underpinned by its close understanding of the local regulatory context and its ability to turn that into a strategic advantage.)

Shoprite, the South Africa–based supermarket chain that now operates more than two thousand stores across the continent, solved distribution challenges by adapting its own centralized distribution model, making it better able to work with both small farmers and international suppliers. By operating its own warehouses, Shoprite stocks up on supplies when prices dip and also keeps enough on hand to avoid stockouts when a disruption occurs upstream in its supply chain. It also makes it easier for its suppliers to deliver their goods, since they don't have to go to each store. Shoprite operates its own fleet for store deliveries, employing sophisticated route-planning technology for maximum efficiency.[5]

As we have noted, many of Africa's successful businesses supply their own electric power and water. Dangote has gone further, partnering with Black Rhino, a subsidiary of the US-based asset manager Blackstone, to develop power-generation projects to feed into Nigeria's grid.[6] Tolaram, the maker of Indomie noodles, has not only developed its own infrastructure but also taken the lead in creating a $1.6 billion public–private partnership to build a new deepwater port near Lagos. SABMiller, too, built its own power grids, waste-treatment plants, and roads. Mark Bowman, the company's former Africa head, says that while that investment pushed up the cost of production, it also created a higher barrier to competitors.

CORNERSTONE 4: UNDERSTAND LOCAL CONTEXT AND CLAIM A PLACE AT THE TABLE WITH GOVERNMENTS

In chapter 1, we celebrated the progress that African governments have made in recent years to improve the ease of doing business in their countries. But there is still a long way to go. Africa's patchwork of regulatory regimes and the gaps that remain in government effectiveness in many parts of the continent present a real challenge to business. As Donald Kaberuka, former president of the African Development Bank, remarked: "Africa's regulatory environment has improved greatly since the 1970s and 1980s, but it is still one of the big risks which every businessman faces."

Companies investing in Africa can't wait until "all the conditions are right for them to do business," in Kaberuka's words. Rather, they need to invest time and effort in understanding the policy and regulatory environment in each country they operate in, building relationships with governments and making sure their voice is heard. The price of failure can be high. Even MTN, Africa's largest mobile phone group, has tripped up: in 2016 it had to pay a $1.7 billion fine in Nigeria after failing to disconnect unregistered SIM cards, as required by that country's regulations. The fine wiped a third off MTN's earnings and caused it to post its first-ever annual loss.

STAYING AHEAD OF AFRICA'S SHIFTING REGULATIONS

Mitchell Elegbe, CEO of Nigeria-based digital-payments company Interswitch, says, "The regulator—not competition—is what keeps me awake at night." He adds: "Regulation, if not properly crafted, can undermine the long-term growth and survival of your business."[7] In fifteen years of successful business in Nigeria, Elegbe has learned some valuable lessons on how to stay ahead of shifting regulation in the financial services and technology sectors. He told us, "You have to find a systematic way of dealing with regulators—although I'd be telling you a lie if I told you I had it all figured out." He explained his tactics: "In Nigeria, I try to have regular quarterly meetings with the regulators to share our view of the payments industry and where we should be going with it in the country. We also try to be as involved as possible in everything the regulators are doing. If they're speaking at a conference, we go and listen. It all takes a long time, but if you get it right it pays off."

How can international companies build the kind of local knowledge such African firms have developed over decades? Our executive survey provides a clue: high-performing companies are twice as likely as lower performers to have local shareholders or board members who help them understand the local context. They are also twice as likely to invest actively in the local communities where they operate, thus improving their chances of being recognized as a good corporate citizen—and so securing a place at the table with government.

Some executives have turned their ability to navigate the intricacies of regulation and government policy into strategic advantage. When Mohammed Dewji joined MeTL, the family business in Tanzania, it was a $30 million trading firm. Since then, it has grown into a $1.5 billion company and the country's largest private-sector employer, with twenty-eight thousand employees. Like so many other small enterprises throughout Africa, MeTL started off by importing finished goods from other markets and selling them locally at a markup. Then, in 1999, in a bid to spur local manufacturing, the Tanzanian government imposed a new set of import taxes ranging from zero percent on raw materials to 10 percent on semiprocessed materials and 25 percent on finished goods—precisely the kinds of goods MeTL traded in.

For many trading companies, this would have been a tremendous setback. Dewji saw it a different way. "It was a huge opportunity," he says. "At that time, everything was imported in this country. And then the government came up with policies that encouraged investment in value addition and job creation."[8] Rather than just pay the new taxes and settle for lower profit margins, Dewji shifted the mix of imports to commodities. And instead of trading these inputs to someone else to use as building blocks for more valuable products, he took MeTL in a whole new direction, building factories to produce his own products. Instead of importing cooking oil, for example, he imported crude palm oil and had MeTL refine its own branded cooking oil. Instead of importing soap, he imported the raw ingredients, and built a factory to make his own.[9]

Similarly, when the Tanzanian government sought to create jobs in the textile industry, it gave preferential tax treatment to local producers while imposing import tariffs of 25 percent on finished goods, along with a value-added tax of 17 percent. MeTL seized the chance to move into textile manufacturing and is now sub-Saharan Africa's largest player operating across the entire value chain. The company has operations in ginning, spinning, weaving, printing, dying, knitting, garmenting, and retailing. The bulk of the goods it produces are for domestic consumption. Says Dewji: "This positions MeTL as the market leader in the textile industry. They (the Chinese) cannot compete with me in my market."[10]

BE A TRUE CORPORATE CITIZEN

Ngozi Okonjo-Iweala told us that she sees community investment as a critical success factor for businesses in Africa. "You need to build trust with whichever community you're in," she said. That starts with being aware of your surroundings, identifying the community's true needs, and thinking big about how to solve them. Said Okonjo-Iweala, "If the community lacks transport and there's a way you can help build a railroad where you are, why not? Because in the end, the community will surround you, protect you, and love you." That, she said, will also help companies build trust with governments.

Just as important, successful global firms have leadership teams that are visibly local and closely connected to the government leaders and business communities in the countries they operate in. As we discuss in chapter 6, that makes the development of local managers and leaders a key priority for business. Expatriates, too, need to make a real effort to integrate into their local communities.

Mark Bowman of SABMiller says it is essential that host countries view your company as a good corporate citizen and a constructive partner to government: "You have to spend more time than you would in other markets explaining the jobs you're creating, your contribution to the tax base, and the steps you are taking to empower locals. In Africa, you shouldn't be seen as someone who's just coming in to assemble your widgets, stretch your profit, and disappear. There are lots of ways you can fail, and that might be one of them." Because duties on beer make up a large proportion of government revenues in many African countries, SABMiller positioned itself as a "co-collector of tax." That gave it a place at the table with senior government leaders and a voice on critical business issues.

GE's company-to-country agreements with the governments of Kenya and Nigeria, discussed in chapter 2, have also given it a place at the table in national discussions on key topics such as infrastructure development. The government leaders we spoke to while writing this book appreciate such approaches. "It's helpful when businesses are honest with government about what's working and what's not," Ngozi Okonjo-Iweala commented. Her advice: if your company is coming up against obstacles to growth, communicate plainly—via your industry association if need be. "Come to government as a group and say, 'Look, we are creating jobs, but you need to give us the space to work effectively.'" Those discussions are not always gentle:

successful companies sometimes need to show "tough love" in their relationships with governments. Aliko Dangote provides a vivid example. After his company bought the Benue cement plant from Nigeria's government in 2002, the government tried to go back on the deal. Dangote stuck it out: "I refused. If I'd allowed somebody else to buy Benue, they would have used it to kill me in the market." After forty-two months of delay, the government finally transferred the plant to Dangote Cement. Later, he sought to break into the cement market in Cameroon, where a government minister was the chairman of his main competitor. The government stopped construction of the Dangote cement plant, in the port of Douala, on the grounds that the land had religious significance for the local community. "They said they used the land to talk to their gods in the water," said Dangote. Again, he did not back down, and succeeded in building a $150 million plant with annual capacity of 1.5 million tons. Years later, when Dangote met Cameroon's president, Paul Biya, at an event in Washington, DC, Biya told him: "I've never seen a fighter like you." Yet Dangote had won the president's respect.

Our focus on the business-government relationship would not be complete without a frank discussion about corruption. The Ibrahim Index shows that while most indicators of good governance have improved over the past decade, corruption measures have deteriorated.[11] Almost half of Africa's countries posted their worst-ever score in this category over the past three years. The consequences go beyond simply the cost of paying a bribe: the direct costs of corruption in Africa are widely estimated at $150 billion per year. To put that in perspective, the cost of providing electricity to all who need it in Africa is estimated at $55 billion per year. Speaking at an anti-corruption meeting in 2015, Akinwumi Adesina, president of the African Development Bank, drew a direct connection between those two facts: "The cost of corruption is massive; it turns the whole continent into darkness."[12]

Our executive survey confirms the seriousness of the problem: one in two respondents cited corruption as a major barrier to business in Africa. Other studies underline how widespread corruption is. In a survey by Afrobarometer, for example, one-third of respondents from thirty-five African countries reported paying a bribe in the previous year to obtain a government service or to pay off the police.[13] Transparency International estimates that 75 million people in Africa have paid a bribe in the past year.[14]

How can companies avoid getting entangled in corruption and play their part in reducing the prevalence of this scourge? Our own approach, and our advice to clients, has been to stick to your values no matter what. For example, when we first set up the McKinsey office in Nigeria, we experienced long delays in securing work permits for expatriate staff. A government official approached us, saying: "If you need to accelerate the process, I can help you." It was a clear solicitation of a bribe. Our response was: "Absolutely not." After that, the permits came through very easily. The would-be bribe takers had evidently come to the conclusion that we would never pay; instead, they decided to focus their time and effort on other companies.

In 2016–2017, we faced a much more painful test of our values—this time in South Africa. The country was rocked by allegations of corruption in government and state-owned enterprises such as Eskom, the national electricity utility. We had served Eskom for years—including helping to end a period of power outages in 2014–2016. We did briefly explore a partnership with a local firm, which we later found to be owned by a questionable character. Though we terminated those discussions, we learned hard lessons from this experience, including the critical need to have the deepest possible understanding of the context of any potential engagement, as well as of the actors involved.

The policy and regulatory playing field in Africa is far from perfect, and there is much that governments need to do to improve the operating environment for business. Yet companies have more room than is often assumed to help improve that environment—and they also have a responsibility to do so. The African Development Bank's Adesina likens the private and public sector to the two wings of a bird: "I've never seen a bird that flies with only one wing. You need both the public sector and the private sector. They are complementary agents of transformation." Although governments have a responsibility to enable business growth—including through providing adequate infrastructure, simplifying regulations, and building a robust legal framework—companies must step up too. Adesina advocates a stronger role for chambers of commerce and other business associations in engaging with governments, communicating businesses' needs, and collaborating to help solve national challenges.

———————

When we interviewed Deepak Singhal, CEO of Tolaram's Dufil Prima Foods, he told us that it takes a "lionheart" to succeed in Africa. Singhal was referring to the courage of the lion, and that is indeed needed, but we would add wisdom, fortitude, and a sense of belonging to a larger community. We've been able to observe many of the most successful businesses on the continent. The one thing they all share is a sober view of Africa's challenges and a mindset that allows them to work around them—and see the business opportunities buried in them.

CHAPTER 6

UNLEASH
AFRICA'S TALENT

As we close our journey though Africa's business revolution, let's make a return visit to Kibera, the massive informal settlement in Nairobi described in chapter 2. You'll see little presence of big business here, yet Kibera teems with entrepreneurial activity. Any possible sliver of value, whether a product or a service, that can be sold or traded is—from use of the primitive toilet facilities to downloads for iPods to guides promising safe passage through the warren of paths that crisscross the settlement. There are tailors, barbers, carpenters, and caterers plying their trades. *The Economist* called Kibera "an African version of a Chinese boomtown, an advertisement for solid human ambition."[1]

For many young residents of Kibera, though, their ambition is to rise out of informality and enter the world of formal business—with all the opportunities for career progression and personal development it represents. That's why, if you visit the local community center any weekday morning, you're likely to find it full to bursting with students of the Generation youth skills program. You might just find some of your next frontline staff there: Generation's purpose is to bridge the gap between youth who lack job training and employers who struggle to find the skills they need for business growth. (Full disclosure: Generation, today a global nonprofit organization, was founded by McKinsey. We continue to support it, alongside major philanthropic groups such as USAID.)

The Kibera center is one of thirty-seven Generation training locations across Kenya. Each offers immersive "boot camp" training programs targeted at building job readiness in areas such as retail and financial sales, customer service, and apparel manufacturing. Not only do these programs teach relevant technical skills, they also use role-play and team exercises to impart behavioral and mindset skills such as punctuality and resilience. For example, a module aimed at building students' sales savvy requires them to sell bottled water on the streets of Kibera and then debrief in their teams about what worked, what didn't, and what to do differently.

By 2017, more than eight thousand young Kenyans had been through a Generation program, and 89 percent of them had found formal employment within three months of graduation. One of them is Stanley, who was born and grew up in Kibera. One of eight children, Stanley was raised by a single mother who often struggled to find money for necessities like food and shelter. Despite performing well in school, Stanley could not find the money to study further. Unable to find full-time employment, Stanley worked odd jobs at a construction site and sold clothes to earn a meager income.

Yet he dreamed of a stable, professional career, and when he heard about Generation, he leaped at the opportunity to join the financial sales program. The skills and confidence he built enabled him to apply for the same jobs as university graduates. Soon after graduation, Stanley received an offer from Old Mutual, a South Africa–based financial services company with operations in many African countries. "After just six weeks I was in a good job as a sales associate. Generation was the platform for me to move from one step to the next," he said.

AFRICA'S TALENT: CONSTRAINT OR OPPORTUNITY?

Africa's growing businesses need talent: among the global and African executives we surveyed, fully half said they expected to expand their African workforces over the next five years. Even in an era of digitization and cost-efficiency, only 2 percent said they planned to reduce their employee numbers. That makes skills shortages a pressing concern. Many African-based companies have reported challenges in attracting and retaining the talent they need to run and grow their businesses. For example, 31 percent of companies surveyed in South Africa in 2015 said they had difficulties filling jobs, despite a national unemployment rate exceeding 25 percent.[2]

Africa's continued underperformance in education is a major factor in such shortages. The average time African children spend in school increased from 3.2 years in 2000 to 5.3 years in 2010, but the rate of improvement has subsequently slowed. To put this into context, children in other emerging regions spend an average of 7.5 to eight years in school. Sub-Saharan Africa's student-teacher ratio in primary schools was forty students per teacher in 2013, almost twice that in other regions. Africa's rate of tertiary education enrollment is half that of India's. Compounding this situation is a brain drain: by one measure, more than 10 percent of Africa's university-educated professionals live and work on other continents.[3]

On the other hand, Africa is generating raw talent on a massive scale. In 2020, it is projected to have a workforce of 504 million–122 million more than in 2010. By 2034, Africa will have more working-age citizens (ages fifteen to sixty-four) than either China or India. By 2050, its working-age population will exceed 1.5 billion (figure 6-1). A large proportion of Africa's workers are young people. And as the stories of Stanley and other Generation graduates show, many of them are bursting with the desire to learn, and the ambition to build stable careers and improve their lives and those of their families.

Increasingly, Africa's business lions are seeing Africa's talent not as a barrier but as an opportunity to unlock. Nicky Newton-King, CEO of the Johannesburg Stock Exchange, told us that many South African companies expanding into the rest of Africa are impressed with the skills and energy of the workforces elsewhere on the continent. "I've never heard talent being raised with me as an issue," she said. In fact, if anything, she's heard the opposite. She adds that, alongside local talent, many African professionals who have studied and worked outside the continent are keen to "come back and do my bit," just as many South Africans exiled during apartheid did after the country's democratization in 1994.

Ashish J. Thakkar of Mara Corporation and Atlas Mara has a similar view: "My personal experience is that talent is a challenge, but it's frankly not as big as people make out. For example, we set up call centers in seven countries across Africa. In six of them, there were no existing call centers—and therefore no talent pools available for the industry. So we put training mechanisms in place, and within a hundred days we had effective call-center agents." For Thakkar, that was a reminder that

FIGURE 6-1

Africa is set to have a larger working-age population than either China or India by 2034

Projected working-age population in key regions,*
billions of people

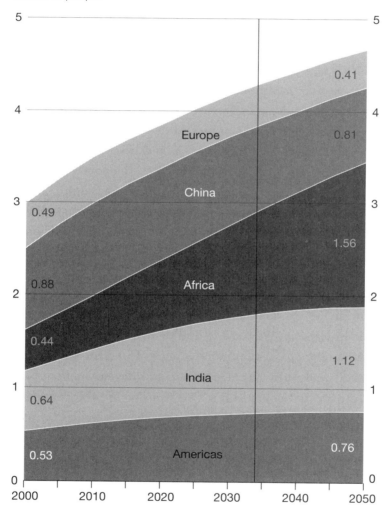

*Working-age population = individuals aged 15–64.

Source: IHS; ILO; McKinsey Global Institute analysis.

Africa has "a population that is educated, entrepreneurial, and eager to learn. If we put in the necessary mechanisms and create the necessary training, you can tap into that very easily. It's not rocket science, and I don't think talent is by any means an excuse not to invest in Africa."

That rings true with our own experience in recruiting and developing talent in Africa. When we opened the McKinsey office in Lagos in 2010, we advertised at university campuses in Nigeria and around the world for top students to join us as entry-level consultants. We received around a thousand applications from Nigerian schools and five hundred from international schools. Many of them were Nigerians and other Africans wanting to come back and contribute to the continent's development, but they also included applicants from Belgium, Brazil, and China. From those five hundred international applicants, we hired twelve people. From the thousand local Nigerian applicants, we hired none—nobody made it through our tests and interviews.

We said to ourselves: "How is this possible? We know the education system has its challenges, but there are lots of smart people in Nigeria. We have to find them and nurture them." So we rethought our recruitment process to better spot people's potential and built more learning and development into our program for new consultants. Our first five local hires went on to top business schools around the world. If we hadn't been willing to look deeper to spot talent, we would have lost out on their contribution.

Fred Swaniker, who founded the African Leadership Academy in 2004 and the African Leadership University in 2013, has interviewed, assessed and developed many more young Africans than we have. "The raw talent in Africa is there in large numbers," he says. "But it just needs to be converted. And that doesn't mean necessarily someone going through a full four-year degree. A three-month or nine-month training program could be enough to unlock the skills that companies need."

Swaniker compares Africa's talent challenges to those of India. "For years, companies in India used to complain, 'The universities are not producing the people we need.' So companies like Infosys created their own corporate academies, and they started training and developing their own people." He adds: "To succeed in Africa, you have to take a more strategic role in developing your own talent. You need to look at talent development as part of your value chain, not as something that is outsourced to the national university system."

By making greater and smarter investments in talent, companies in Africa will also play their part in turning Africa's demographic boom into shared prosperity. The International Monetary Fund estimates that Africa needs to create 18 million high-productivity jobs each year until 2035 to maximize the economic benefits of its population growth—an unprecedented level of job growth. Youth unemployment today officially stands at around 10 percent in sub-Saharan Africa, but many more young people are in "vulnerable employment"; that is, they get by in informal or temporary jobs that offer little security or potential for career development. As Africa's youth demographic grows, providing stable jobs that offer a path for advancement is imperative for the continent's economic future.

In chapter 3, we profiled the remarkable pan-African growth story of Saham, the Morocco-based insurer. It turns out that talent strategy is an essential component of its success. Nadia Fettah, Saham's CEO, told us she spends one-third of her time on talent management and development. Other CEOs we interviewed put equally heavy emphasis on finding, developing, motivating, and managing their people. But what are the components of an effective African talent strategy, and what are the practical steps that businesses should take to make that strategy succeed? We advocate three talent imperatives for Africa:

1. Find smart ways to build vocational skills among entry-level and frontline workers.

2. Create robust internal talent-development processes to grow your talent from within.

3. Harness the power of inclusion—particularly the opportunity to boost women's participation and advancement in the workplace.

TALENT IMPERATIVE 1: BUILD VOCATIONAL SKILLS FOR FRONTLINE EMPLOYEES

Data from Egypt, Morocco, and South Africa indicate that by 2021, between 41 percent and 50 percent of jobs will fall into a category that McKinsey Global Institute characterizes as "skilled entry-level," which includes administrators, craftspeople, and operators.[4] These roles require practical, on-the-job skills building combined with theoretical training. Unfortunately, most young Africans are not offered such training. For example, only 8 percent of African students in secondary education were enrolled in vocational programs in 2015, compared with 18 percent in East Asia and the Pacific and 17 percent in OECD countries. Africa also lags other regions in tertiary education enrollment (figure 6-2).

FIGURE 6-2

Africans' enrollment in tertiary and vocational education is low compared with other regions

Students enrolled in tertiary education by region, %

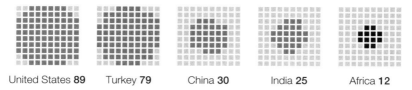

| United States **89** | Turkey **79** | China **30** | India **25** | Africa **12** |

Students in secondary education enrolled in vocational programs by region, %

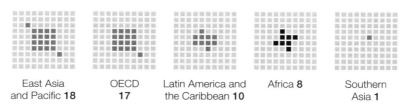

| East Asia and Pacific **18** | OECD **17** | Latin America and the Caribbean **10** | Africa **8** | Southern Asia **1** |

Students in secondary education enrolled in vocational programs in African countries, %

| Egypt **22** | Rwanda **14** | Algeria **8** | S. Africa **7** | Morocco **6** |

Source: World Bank education indicators; McKinsey Global Institute analysis.

The result is that many of Africa's fast-growing businesses struggle to find entry-level employees with the skills they need. One of them is Subway, the global quick-service restaurant chain, which sees Africa as a key growth opportunity as it shifts its footprint toward emerging markets. Alex Brand, an executive at Subway's Kenyan franchise holder, told us that hundreds of young people apply each week for positions at the company's sandwich shops. "People drop résumés at all our outlets," he said. "They somehow find our main office and convince the guard that they have an appointment and come up and drop their résumés there too. So there are a lot of young people that really want these jobs."

But most of them "don't know what it means to have a full-time job and don't understand the standards we demand here," Brand said. Out of every hundred job-seekers, only two or three make it through Subway's recruitment process—wasting precious human resources time. Even among those who do make the cut, retention has been a problem. "In our business, high turnover is bad: new employees don't know the systems, aren't comfortable talking with customers, and need training," Brand told us.

Gilbert Cheruiyot, founder of Gilchery Skip-Trace, faced similar problems. His business has filled a gap in Kenya's burgeoning consumer market: the need to manage customers who get behind with payments on their credit cards, car loans, or store credit. Since its launch in 2011, Gilchery has signed on several of Kenya's largest banks as customers. The company has needed to recruit dozens of agents to its call centers, but has struggled to find people with the right skills. "Our biggest challenge has been to find the right staff," Cheruiyot said. "Most young graduates don't have the tolerance and emotional intelligence to deal with indebted customers, who can be highly uncooperative. Our agents need to be able to calm them down and strike a deal." He too faced high levels of staff turnover: "For every five people I employed, I'd be left with only one after two or three months. It was very frustrating, because we'd spent a lot of time and resources training them."

Subway and Gilchery needed a solution that would match their job openings with young job-seekers who had the right skills and workplace aptitude. That led them, along with 180 other employers, to hire from Generation Kenya. At Subway

Kenya, for example, around 40 percent of local staff are Generation graduates. Partnering with Generation has greatly improved the company's hiring "hit rate," reduced shrinkage, and boosted employee retention. Several Generation graduates have been promoted to managerial positions. One, Stellah Jepkemboi, was appointed an assistant manager in 2017 at the age of twenty-one. She credits Generation with teaching her how to handle people—a critical skill in the restaurant business: "If a customer is upset, I now know how to stay calm, actually listen to them, and offer them a solution."

In Gilchery's case, Generation provided the company with job-ready call-center agents—people who have "the right attitude, high tolerance levels, and the ability to put up with anything and still remain composed," in Cheruiyot's words. They are also fast learners, he says: "Their productivity is improving month after month. We are able to make more collections than before, which is making our clients happy." After hiring forty of the program's graduates, Gilchery engaged Generation to develop a customized training for the company.

Generation provides heartening evidence that young Africans entering the workforce for the first time have what it takes to become high-performing employees in modern businesses. All that's needed is a smart approach to preparing them for the world of work. Generation is one such approach, but there are others with strong track records, such as South Africa's Harambee Youth Employment Accelerator. Moreover, Africa's most successful companies are increasingly making vocational training—whether outsourced or insourced—a core part of how they do business. One example is Aviation Industry Corporation of China (AVIC), a diversified Chinese state-owned enterprise that has its roots in aviation but also has manufacturing, services, and construction business units. AVIC has set up technical and vocational training programs in six African countries to develop the skills needed not only for its own subsidiaries but also for other Chinese companies.

In Gabon, for example, the company has set up training programs focused on machinery, electronics, aeronautical maintenance, and skills for the country's petroleum and timber industries. It has also partnered with African governments to launch the Africa Tech Challenge, a competition aimed at building technical skills such as machining and mobile app development. Initially focused on Kenya, the contest now also covers Ghana, Uganda, and Zambia. The winners receive cash rewards and offers for full-time employment with AVIC.[5]

TALENT IMPERATIVE 2: CREATE ROBUST INTERNAL PROCESSES TO GROW TALENT FROM WITHIN

Getting job-ready frontline staff is one challenge, but finding and developing employees with technical, managerial, and leadership skills is an even more complex undertaking. In our survey of African and global business, 27 percent of respondents said they faced pressing challenges in finding experienced technical workers, while nearly the same number said they struggled to find appropriately skilled senior managers and frontline supervisors. For example, e-commerce company Jumia has found it difficult to recruit middle managers. "This is the critical role when it comes to talent," said Sacha Poignonnec, Jumia's CEO. "But it's very difficult for us to find people who are good at managing a team of ten people." Many businesses also said they faced gaps in digital talent. Gro Intelligence, the Nairobi-based technology startup, is one such firm. CEO Sara Menker remarked: "We get a massive influx of résumés for software engineers, but very few make it through our technical screening process. It's a very, very young market." She added: "When we do find talent that makes it through our hiring process, they are world-class."

A pessimistic view of these talent gaps would suggest that businesses in Africa should embark on a "war for talent," outbidding one another for scarce technical and managerial skills. Certainly, successful companies need to shape and communicate compelling employee value propositions. Mobile operator MTN, for example, created the "MTN Deal," which includes a promise of employee development, celebrating diversity, competitive reward, and recognition.[6] Companies also need to tailor such value propositions to different talent segments, ranging from global highfliers in the African diaspora to local hires with rapid advancement potential.

But a more optimistic view—one we share—holds that companies can grow the leaders, managers, and specialists they need from within their organizations. Competition for talent will remain a daily reality, but smart investment in people development is the true differentiator of companies that win in Africa. Indeed, that recognition is at the heart of employee value propositions like MTN's: it emphasizes mentorship, coaching, and training just as much as compensation.

Arguably, Africa is at the early stages of a corporate education revolution, with many companies investing heavily in internal training programs and institutes. Among high-performing firms in our executive survey, more than 60 percent run such programs in their African operations (figure 6-3). The Dangote Group, for example, established the Dangote Academy in 2010 to train employees in technical and managerial skills, on the explicit recognition that "we cannot rely on universities and colleges to provide the very specialized technical and managerial training required to run major industrial factories such as ours, particularly in the large numbers of such people that we will need."[7]

FIGURE 6-3

High-performing companies are investing heavily in developing local talent

Our Africa business survey underlines the importance of training and apprenticeship.

What practices does your organization use to source and develop talent in Africa?[1] % of respondents

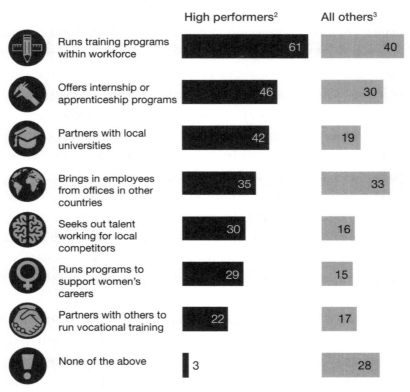

	High performers[2]	All others[3]
Runs training programs within workforce	61	40
Offers internship or apprenticeship programs	46	30
Partners with local universities	42	19
Brings in employees from offices in other countries	35	33
Seeks out talent working for local competitors	30	16
Runs programs to support women's careers	29	15
Partners with others to run vocational training	22	17
None of the above	3	28

[1]Respondents who answered "other" or "don't know" are not shown. Question was asked only of those who said they have been to at least one country in Africa, that 5% or more of their organizations' current revenue is earned in Africa, and that their organizations operate in at least one African country.
[2]Respondents in high-performing companies, n = 166.
[3]Respondents in all other companies n = 603.

Source: McKinsey Insights executive survey on business in Africa, 2017.

But there is clearly room to expand such efforts, and to increase their impact. Nadia Fettah told us that Saham Finances struggles to spend its full training budget—because it is difficult to find training providers across African markets who meet the insurer's standards. "We find the external training offers poor, so we have to build our own solutions internally." Sacha Poignonnec of Jumia has had the same experience, despite "looking constantly" for training providers to invest in. To close the gap in middle-management skills, Jumia has created an internal program covering topics such as time management, priority management, and how to manage a team effectively.

Several of Africa's leading companies have gone a step further and created in-depth development programs for high-potential employees. (Such internship programs are a differentiator of success among high-performing firms in our executive survey.) GE, for example, runs a year-long "early career development program" for the recent university graduates it hires in Africa. As Jay Ireland, GE's Africa president, pointed out to us: "When you're hiring young people out of university in the US, almost every one of them has interned somewhere, so they know what a corporate environment is like. In Africa, that's generally not the case. Our program helps solve that—and we've had very good success. Many of our graduates have gone on and done very well in higher roles."

Smaller companies can adopt similar approaches. Brooks Washington, CEO of Roha Ventures, struggled to find engineers with the right skill set to build and operate its state-of-the-art glass bottle factory in Ethiopia. "We've found great people who are clearly very capable. But it's rare that you find someone who's a perfect fit, especially when you're building something that's never been done before. So we recruited strong local engineers, then added a budget to take them to South Africa to train them for six months. It's expensive, but it will give us a completely trained local workforce with the best glass manufacturing skills in the world."

Mark Bowman, former Africa CEO of SABMiller, has a name for this international training and development approach: *industrial tourism.* He told us: "We would take a unit manager from one of our breweries in Nigeria, for example, to work with colleagues in Colombia or Peru for a few weeks. It was a transformative experience—they'd return fired up. It was a great way to tap into the intrinsics of people's motivation."

In fact, the companies leading the way in talent development are making geographic mobility a requirement for career advancement at senior levels—a key step in building a pan-African business with shared values and practices. Saham has instituted a rule that, in any given African country, the deputy CEO of its local operation can never be the next country CEO. "That pushes people toward greater mobility," said CEO Nadia Fettah. "You can grow in your own country, but if one day you want to have the number-one position, you need to travel."

Together, these talent-development processes are creating a new generation of savvy, energized business managers and operators across the continent. Africa's business growth will itself help to close the talent gap by creating opportunities for young Africans to build their skills, advance their careers, and become leaders. One example is Mary Karuthai. She works at the Kenyan subsidiary of the Chinese broadcasting company StarTimes, which has risen rapidly to become one of the largest pay-television providers in Africa. In 2010, two years after graduating from the University of Nairobi with a commerce degree, she joined the company as a customer service representative. By 2017, she had risen through the ranks to become the assistant director of operations, overseeing some four hundred employees across several departments, including after-sales service, maintenance, and the company's call center. "StarTimes is giving many people opportunities to grow fast in their careers," Karuthai said. "If you look at the managers here, you'll see that most of them are young people."

TALENT IMPERATIVE 3: HARNESS THE POWER OF INCLUSION—PARTICULARLY WOMEN'S ADVANCEMENT

In corporate Africa, stories of women's advancement like that of Karuthai are unfortunately still quite rare. As part of McKinsey's global "Women Matter" initiative, we undertook a major research effort on women's participation in business and government in Africa. We found that, despite progress in recent years, there is a large gap to close.[8]

In the African companies we surveyed as part of that effort, women accounted for 47 percent of nonmanagement professional positions. At the middle-management level, this figure fell to 40 percent and at senior management level to 29 percent. From start to end, this amounts to "leakage" of 18 percentage points. In these companies, women made up 45 percent of the workforce but received just 36 percent of promotions. Some companies manage to promote women into middle-management roles but then encounter difficulties promoting them to senior management positions. Women are effectively locked out of the top.

As a result, Africa has far too few women CEOs. At executive committee level, women hold 23 percent of positions in corporate Africa. At CEO level, though, they hold just 5 percent of positions. Although that makes Africa the top-performing region alongside the United States, it's far from satisfactory if the pool of senior executives from which CEOs are typically selected is nearly one-quarter female. At board level, African women hold just 14 percent of seats.

In corporate Africa, most women managers hold staff roles such as HR and legal, rather than the line roles that offer more exposure to decision-making forums, core operations, and promotion to CEO positions. In the companies surveyed, 56 percent of female senior managers hold staff roles, and there is a substantial pay gap between men and women holding senior positions in private-sector companies—arguably another indicator of women's lack of influence. In South Africa, for example, women board members earn 17 percent less than their male counterparts.

Despite the strong business case for gender diversity in leadership, only 31 percent of the African companies we surveyed saw it as a top strategic priority for the CEO, while 25 percent thought it was of no importance. That is a major missed opportunity for business: globally, McKinsey's research shows that companies with a greater share of women on their boards of directors and executive committees tend to perform better financially.[9] African companies are no different; we found that the earnings before interest and taxes (EBIT) margin of those with at least a quarter share of women on their boards was on average 20 percent higher than the industry average (figure 6-4).

"Introducing more women at leadership level simply introduces broader perspectives and new ways to manage problems,"

FIGURE 6-4

A link between gender diversity and profit margins creates a sound business case for women's advancement

Women's representation on the boards of African companies versus EBIT[1] margin deviation from industry average.

Diversity and EBIT by business quartile,[2] %

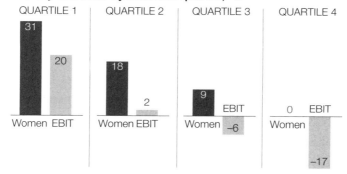

Women's representation on the ExCos of African companies versus EBIT margin deviation from industry average.[3]

Representation and EBIT by business quartile, %

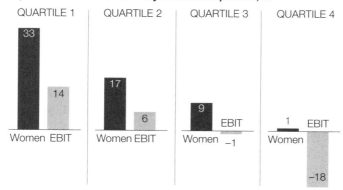

[1] Earnings before interest and taxes.
[2] A quartile is defined as each of four equal groups into which a population can be divided according to the distribution of values of a particular variable.
Total number of companies in sample = 210.
[3] 2010 to 2014; GSMA Mobile Money Deployment Tracker.

Source: Orbis database, 2014; company annual reports and websites.

said a Moroccan executive interviewed for our Women Matter study. "Diversity is key for a successful organization. It also allows companies and public entities to tap into the entire talent pool rather than deprive themselves of half of it." That holds true not just for companies but for entire economies. Our analysis suggests that if women participated in the economy identically to men, they could add more than $300 billion to sub-Saharan Africa's annual GDP by 2025.

Graça Machel, an international human rights advocate, has made women's empowerment in Africa one of her core missions. Among other initiatives, her Graça Machel Trust houses New Faces New Voices, which advocates for women's access to finance and financial services and aims to bridge the funding gap in financing women-owned businesses in Africa. The program also pushes for policy and legislative changes to increase financial inclusion and bring more women into the formal financial system. Machel urges both male and female business leaders to make women's advancement "part and parcel of your strategy of growth and sustainability for the next five, ten, fifteen, twenty years." As she told us: "You need to value diversity as an element of strength, and make it part of a cultural, institutional transformation. Human resources departments and CEOs need to make upward mobility for female staff part of HR strategy and succession planning, and ask themselves: 'How can we get more qualified women into the C-suite? How are we nurturing our female talent? How do we ensure more capable women are sitting at the highest levels of decision making?'"

Phumzile Mlambo-Ngcuka, former deputy president of South Africa and now United Nations undersecretary-general and executive director of UN Women, echoes these views. She argues that African companies must take decisive action to fix the "broken ladder" of women's advancement, including by challenging unconscious bias in their organizations. "Even now, when we see more women graduating with the same qualifications as men, there's still a preference for men in many companies," she told us. "Because a guys' club has formed, and it's tight. They prefer to hire people who look like them and perpetuate the stereotype that men make better leaders. This is the way society has been structured: patriarchy is an affirmative system for men."

One way to break this cycle, in Mlambo-Ngcuka's view, is for companies to set aspirational quotas for women's representation at board and executive committee level. High-potential women managers also need active sponsors and mentors—people whose philosophy is "I've got you, I've got your back," in Mlambo-Ngcuka's words. To unlock the power of gender equality in business, leadership is needed from both women and men. Mlambo-Ngcuka is encouraged that "we're seeing more men who care about gender equality, who ask the right questions, and advocate for change."

Those steps are critical if Africa is to unlock the talent and leadership needed to reach its full potential. Companies in Africa need to make gender diversity a top board and CEO priority and to develop a cohesive gender diversity transformation strategy—one based on solid metrics including pay levels of female versus male staff, women's attrition rates and reasons for exiting, and the percentage of women receiving promotions. At McKinsey, we are driving our own transformation: the proportion of women in our global incoming consulting class has risen from 29 percent to 38 percent in five years. We, like many organizations, have much more to do.

Across Africa, many pioneering companies are adopting innovative approaches to convert the energy of Africa's young talent—male and female—into productive, skilled workforces.

Some have built sophisticated internal academies; others have helped cocreate multicompany programs such as Generation; while others are working directly with state education systems to improve quality and shift their focus to more work-relevant skills. In doing so, they are building a powerful source of sustainable growth for their own companies. Indeed, we believe that wise investment in talent development is perhaps the single most important step that any company can take to succeed in Africa.

DO WELL BY DOING GOOD

We have had the privilege to meet and work with many remarkable businesspeople, from every corner of the globe, who have built successful enterprises in Africa. Each of those companies has adopted strategies that include all or most of the imperatives we've spelled out in this book. They've set out bold visions for growth. They've spotted and acted on favorable long-term trends—and recast Africa's challenges as opportunities—ahead of the competition. They've drawn a map of Africa around the most promising countries and cities. They've made smart moves to innovate their product and service offerings, harness technology, and drive up productivity. They've managed Africa's volatility by building resilience into their business models. And they've invested in talent, bringing out the best in Africa's people.

What has struck us time and again in these conversations, though, is how many of Africa's successful business leaders are driven by a deeper purpose. They look at Africa's high levels of poverty; its gaps in infrastructure, education, and health care; and its governance problems, and they don't just see barriers to business, but human issues they feel responsible for solving.

Consider the example of Strive Masiyiwa, chairman of the pan-African telecom, media, and technology company Econet Group. There is no doubting his business ambitions: he is the major shareholder in fast-growing Liquid Telecom, now Africa's largest broadband infrastructure and data services company. In 2017, he launched a new media business, Kwesé, which enables African viewers to stream Netflix and view premium content on their mobile phones for as little as $10 a month. But Masiyiwa has put equal energy into his philanthropic initiatives: for example, he has used his wealth to provide scholarships to more than 250,000 young Africans over the past twenty years. He also devotes an enormous amount of energy to mentoring the next generation of African entrepreneurs, including through regular posts on his Facebook page, which has over 3 million followers.

As Masiyiwa explained to us, these twin passions stem from a simple philosophy: "To be successful, you need to be more than a businessman—you need to be a responsible citizen. Africa is a continent with extraordinary challenges, and it's a cop-out just to wait for governments to deal with them. If you see a problem, then think about how you can solve a piece of it." He shared the example of a cholera outbreak in one of the countries in which Econet operates. His local office told him that people were dying because they lacked the necessary medicines, and government processes to procure them were slow. "Then and there, I arranged for the medicines to be airlifted in," he told us. Masiyiwa has helped in other emergency situations too, including the Ebola epidemic that struck West Africa in 2014–2015.

But what really animates his initiatives in education and entrepreneurship—as well as his technology businesses—is a desire to move the needle on Africa's long-term challenges. As he told us, "The exciting part is asking, 'What is the root cause of this problem? What can we do to address that root cause?'"

That's a question that all business leaders operating in Africa, wherever their company's headquarters might be, would do well to answer. That kind of enlightened problem solving has motivated a cohort of young Western entrepreneurs—such as Jesse Moore of M-Kopa and Sacha Poignonnec of Jumia—to build some very innovative African businesses. As Moore told us, his purpose is to have M-Kopa's solar-power kits "revolutionize the lives of millions of people in Africa, just as mobile telephony and mobile money have done."

Big multinationals such as Coca-Cola and GE also see their business objectives and social purpose as intertwined. An example, mentioned earlier, is GE's collaboration with the government of Nigeria to support the upgrade of infrastructure and public health services. Though GE has built profitable businesses through this relationship, its commitment goes far deeper. The company is also helping to build science and technology skills across the continent, including by supporting curriculum development at several African universities. "We believe that multinationals have a key role to play in investing in the infrastructure of skills-building," GE's Africa president and CEO, Jay Ireland, told us.

For many companies operating in Africa, contributing to the social and economic development of the countries they operate in follows naturally from their long-term growth strategies. Very often, it also requires them to engage in a robust manner with governments. Nigeria's recent improvement in the World Bank's ease-of-doing-business ranking, for example, is due in part to businesses in that country speaking up about the challenges they faced in bureaucratic red tape, moving goods across borders, and obtaining visas for staff visiting from other countries—and working actively with the government to address those barriers. In South Africa, many of the country's largest companies convened in 2016 to tackle the problem of the country's sluggish growth and high unemployment, creating the SA SME Fund with the government's support. The fund, financed by an initial contribution of over $100 million from participating companies, invests in smaller businesses that are scalable and able to contribute to economic growth and job creation.[1]

All in all, we are convinced that any company seeking to build a sustainable, scalable business in Africa needs to focus on creating value for both shareholders and stakeholders. There is no inherent tension between earning healthy profits and serving the interests of employees, suppliers, customers, creditors, communities, and the environment.[2] Africa is a continent where, perhaps more than anywhere else, business can do well by doing good. Those who focus on fulfilling a major unmet need—as Equity Bank has done for people excluded from financial services and MTN has done for people without telephones—stand to earn outsized returns for their shareholders while having a transformative impact on society.

Tony Elumelu, founder of Nigeria-based United Bank for Africa and today a leading philanthropist, believes this transformative power of the private sector can be magnified many times. He espouses the philosophy of "Africapitalism"—which includes a commitment to long-term investment and the creation of both economic prosperity and social wealth. As Elumelu told us, "Government simply cannot deliver the enormous growth in employment that is Africa's biggest challenge and greatest opportunity. But equally, business needs to understand its responsibilities and acknowledge that returns go beyond just the bottom line."

We heartily concur with the analysis of Fred Swaniker, founder of the African Leadership University: "The companies that have done well historically, and the ones that will continue to do well, are taking a holistic view to their role in society," he told us. "They realize it's actually in your shareholders' interest that you are seen to be contributing to the development of the country, whether through education or building infrastructure or giving other forms of value that make you a great corporate citizen and national asset."

Graça Machel advocates a "social compact" that would see governments, the private sector, academia, and civil society organizations agree on shared responsibilities to solve Africa's biggest social and economic challenges and meet the UN's Sustainable Development Goals. As she told us, "Those goals are an ambitious, universal call to end poverty, protect the environment, and ensure that all members of our global family enjoy peace and prosperity. They require that we 'leave no one behind.'" She sees a central role for the private sector to partner in poverty-eradication efforts and collaborate with the public sector and civil society to drive job creation on a massive scale. Machel believes business leaders should ask themselves, "If our country has a certain percentage of young people who are unemployed, what kind of creative, forward-thinking changes do we have to implement to accelerate job-creation and increase employment opportunities for our youth? How can we move from producing five thousand jobs a year to 2 million a year, for example?" Such audacious goals, she said, "require a change in mindset in all of us. Entire industries and leaders themselves have to meaningfully transform—it can no longer be business as usual." Machel's late husband, Nelson Mandela, would have agreed. In his autobiography, *Long Walk to Freedom*, he wrote: "There is no passion to be found playing small—in settling for a life that is less than the one you are capable of living."[3]

We give the last word to one of the doyens of African business, Manu Chandaria—a leader who embodies the approach to life that Mandela espoused. He is the chairman of the Comcraft Group, a multibillion-dollar manufacturing and technology company with operations in forty countries. He is also a noted philanthropist and the founding chairman of the East African Business Council and the Kenya Private Sector Alliance. His achievements have been recognized by Queen Elizabeth II, who named him a member of the Order of the British Empire, and the president of Kenya, who bestowed on him the honor of Chief of the Order of Burning Spear.

"The whole point is to have a longer-term vision besides making money," Chandaria told us. If you want to succeed in Africa, he said, then your approach needs to be, "I don't only want to earn my living, I want to make things good for the people who work for me and the community I live in. It's not just about corporate social responsibility—that kind of philosophy needs to be built in your approach to business."

NOTES

PREFACE

1. Jacques Bughin et al., *Lions on the Move II: Realizing the Potential of Africa's Economies*, McKinsey Global Institute, September 2016.

2. Mutsa Chironga et al., *Roaring to Life: Growth and Innovation in African Retail Banking*, McKinsey & Company, February 2018.

3. Mutsa Chironga, Hilary De Grandis, and Yassir Zouaoui, "Mobile Financial Services in Africa: Winning the Battle for the Customer," McKinsey & Company, September 2017.

4. Figures based on McKinsey analysis of data from Analysys Mason (http://www.analysysmason.com) and Dataxis (http://dataxis.com).

5. Figures based on McKinsey analysis of data from Analysys Mason (http://www.analysysmason.com).

6. Alexandra Dumitru and Raphie Hayat, "Sub-Saharan Africa: Politically More Stable, but Still Fragile," RaboResearch—Economic Research, Rabobank, December 3, 2015; Peter Dörrie, "The Wars Ravaging Africa in 2016," *The National Interest*, January 22, 2016.

7. *While Poverty in Africa Has Declined, Number of Poor Has Increased*, World Bank, March 2016, http://www.worldbank.org/en/region/afr/publication/poverty-rising-africa-poverty-report.

8. "Africa Literacy Facts," African Library Project, https://www.africanlibraryproject.org/our-african-libraries/africa-facts.

9. The studies we drew on include the McKinsey Global Institute reports Charles Roxburgh, et al., *Lions on the Move: The Progress and Potential of African Economies* (June 2010); David Fine, et al., *Africa at Work: Job Creation and Inclusive Growth* (August 2012); James Manyika et al., *Lions Go Digital: The Internet's Transformative Potential in Africa* (November 2013), and *Lions on the Move II*; and the McKinsey reports *The Rise of the African Consumer* (November 2012); Antonio Castellano et al., *Brighter Africa: The Growth Potential of the Sub-Saharan Electricity Sector* (February 2015); Lohini Moodley et al., *Women Matter Africa* (August 2016); and Irene Yuan Sun, Kartik Jayaram, and Omid Kassiri, *Dance of the Lions and Dragons: How Are Africa and China Engaging, and How Will the Partnership Evolve?* (2017).

10. Monique Vanek, "Inside Billionaire Aliko Dangote's $12bn Dangote Oil Refinery," *CNBC Africa*, June 27, 2017.

11. Bloomberg Markets, "Africa's Richest Man Has a Plan: Cement, Then Oil—Then Arsenal FC," August 17, 2017.

CHAPTER 1

1. C. I. Jones, "The Facts of Economic Growth," *Handbook of Macroeconomics*, vol. 2A (Amsterdam: Elsevier BV, 2016).

2. Charles Roxburgh et al., *Lions on the Move: The Progress and Potential of African Economies*, McKinsey Global Institute, June 2010.

3. Joseph Cotterill and David Pilling, "South Africa and Nigeria Limp out of Recession," *Financial Times*, September 5, 2017.

4. Tim McConnell, "What's the World's Fastest-Growing Economy? Ghana Contends for the Crown," *New York Times*, March 10, 2018.

5. McKinsey global citizen survey, 2017.

6. See Peter Bisson, Rik Kirkland, and Elizabeth Stephenson, "The Great Rebalancing," McKinsey & Company, June 2010, https://www.mckinsey.com/business-functions/strategy-and-corporate-finance/our-insights/the-great-rebalancing.

7. Ezra Greenberg, Martin Hirt, and Sven Smit, "The Global Forces Inspiring a New Narrative of Progress," *McKinsey Quarterly*, April 2017.

8. *Doing Business 2018: Reforming to Create Jobs*, World Bank, October 31, 2017.

9. *Doing Business 2014 Economy Profile: Rwanda*, World Bank Group, 2013, https://openknowledge.worldbank.org/handle/10986/18880.

10. Jacques Bughin et al., *Lions on the Move II: Realizing the Potential of Africa's Economies*, McKinsey Global Institute, September 2016.

11. Calestous Juma and Francis Mangeni, "The Benefits of Africa's New Free Trade Area," Harvard Kennedy School Belfer Center, June 11, 2015, https://www.belfercenter.org/publication/benefits-africas-new-free-trade-area-0.

12. Tania Holt, Mehdi Lahrichi, and Jorge Santos da Silva, *Africa: A Continent of Opportunity for Pharma and Patients*, McKinsey & Company, June 2015.

13. *Aspen Integrated Report 2017*, Aspen Pharma, June 2017, https://www.aspenpharma.com/wp-content/uploads/2017/11/Aspen-2017-Integrated-Report-LR.pdf.

14. Ethiopian Airlines Factsheet—April 2018, https://www.ethiopianairlines.com/Cms_Data/Contents/EthiopianAirlines/Media/Corporate/FactSheet/Ethiopian-short-FactSheet-April-2018.pdf.

15. John Aglionby, "Ethiopian Airlines Soars with Help from the State," *Financial Times*, February 9, 2016.

16. Kaleyesus Bekele, "The Rise and Rise of Asky Airlines . . . with More to Come," *African Aerospace Online News Service*, September 6, 2016.

17. Jacques Bughin et al., *Lions on the Move II: Realizing the Potential of Africa's Economies*, McKinsey Global Institute, September 2016.

18. This analysis excludes state-owned enterprises and multinational corporations.

19. The total revenue pool is 90 percent of what it could be when South African companies are included.

20. Jake Bright, "An e-Commerce Challenge in Africa: Selling to People Who Aren't Online," *The New Yorker*, June 30, 2016.

21. Ibid.

22. Yolandi Groenewald, "Matlare's Nigerian Waterloo," *City Press*, November 22, 2015; Ann Crotty, "Dangote Finally Turns Corner," *Business Day*, April 18, 2017.

23. Mutsa Chironga et al., *Roaring to Life: Growth and Innovation in African Retail Banking*, McKinsey & Company, February 2018.

24. Chris Bradley, Martin Hirt, and Sven Smit, *Strategy Beyond the Hockey Stick: People, Probabilities, and Big Moves to Beat the Odds* (Hoboken, NJ: John Wiley & Sons, Inc., 2018).

25. David White, Mehrdad Baghai, and Stephen Coley, *The Alchemy of Growth: Practical Insights for Building the Enduring Enterprise* (New York: Perseus Books, 1999).

26. https://www.mckinsey.com/business-functions/strategy-and-corporate-finance/how-we-help-clients/growth-and-innovation.

CHAPTER 2

1. James Manyika et al., *Digital Finance for All: Powering Inclusive Growth in Emerging Economies*, McKinsey Global Institute, September 2016.

2. Samuel Gebre, "Interswitch Nigeria Sees Delayed IPO Concluded by End-2019," *Bloomberg*, September 14, 2017.

3. James Manyika et al., *Digital Finance for All*.

4. Jacques Bughin et al., *Lions on the Move II: Realizing the Potential of Africa's Economies*, McKinsey Global Institute, September 2016.

5. Ibid.

6. United Nations population division database, http://www.un.org/en/development/desa/population/publications/database/index.shtml.

7. See, for example, Paul Collier, *African Urbanization: An Analytic Policy Guide*, International Growth Centre working paper, 2016.

8. Bughin et al., *Lions on the Move II*.

9. Ibid.

10. Lal K. Almas and Oladipo Obembe, "Agribusiness Model in Africa: A Case Study of Zambeef Products PLC," *International Food and Agribusiness Management Review* 17, special issue B (2014).

11. Katrina Manson, "Nestlé Cuts Africa Workforce as Middle Class Growth Disappoints," *Financial Times*, June 16, 2015.

12. Leonie Barrie, "How Ethiopia's Flagship Textile and Apparel Park Is Taking Shape," just-style.com, May 5, 2017; www.skyscrapercity.com.

13. Other African countries, however, may struggle to compete against low labor costs in Asian countries such as Bangladesh. See Alan Gelb et al., *Can Africa Be a Manufacturing Destination? Labor Costs in Comparative Perspective* (Washington, DC: Center for Global Development, October 2017).

14. Bughin et al., *Lions on the Move II*.

15. Ibid.

16. Omono Eremionkhale, "GZ Industries Will Open SH1.3 Billion Sultan Hamud Plant in 2016," *Venturesafrica*, November 6, 2015; Janice Kew, "Nigerian Firm Takes on Nampak," *IOL Business Report*, September 30, 2015; Dinfin Mulupi, "Nigerian Manufacturer Cashing in on Demand for Drinks in Africa," *How We Made It in Africa*, March 27, 2014, https://www.howwemadeitinafrica.com/nigerian-aluminium-can-manufacturer-cashing-in-on-demand-for-drinks-in-africa/.

17. Irene Yuan Sun, Kartik Jayaram, and Omid Kassiri, *Dance of the Lions and Dragons: How Are Africa and China Engaging, and How Will the Partnership Evolve?* McKinsey & Company, June 2017.

18. Bughin et al., *Lions on the Move II*.

19. Ibid.

20. Ibid.

21. The World Bank has highlighted this type of manufacturing as a particularly exciting and viable opportunity for Africa, especially given increasing costs and regulatory complexity in China. See Hinh T. Dinh et al., *Light Manufacturing in Africa: Targeted Policies to Enhance Private Investment and Create Jobs*, Africa Development Forum, World Bank, 2012.

22. These wages are an average for the entire Chinese economy and are estimated from data on total wages plus benefits divided by total employment. The data come from the Global Growth Model of McKinsey & Company's Strategy & Trend Analysis Center.

23. Bughin et al., *Lions on the Move II*.

24. Irene Yuan Sun, "The World's Next Great Manufacturing Center," *Harvard Business Review*, May–June 2017, 122–129.

25. Lily Kuo and Abdi Latif Dahir, "Alibaba's Jack Ma Says African Entrepreneurs Should Learn from Failure Not Success," *Quartz Africa*, July 20, 2017.

26. Kevin Watkins, "Imagine Life Without Electricity—That's the Reality for Two-Thirds of Africa and the Results Are Devastating," *Independent*, June 5, 2015, http://www.independent.co.uk/voices/comment/imagine-life-without-electricity-thats-the-reality-for-two-thirds-of-africa-and-the-results-are-10300033.html.

27. Favour Nnabugwu, "'We Spend N8bn on Diesel Annually,' says MTN Nigeria," *Vanguard*, June 24, 2015.

28. Clayton M. Christensen, Efosa Ojomo, and Derek van Bever, "Africa's New Generation of Innovators," *Harvard Business Review*, January–February 2017, 128–136.

29. Antonio Castellano et al., *Brighter Africa: The Growth Potential of the Sub-Saharan Electricity Sector*, McKinsey & Company, February 2015.

30. Richard Dobbs et al., *Infrastructure Productivity: How to Save $1 Trillion a Year*, McKinsey Global Institute, January 2013.

31. www.ge.com/africa/company/nigeria.

32. https://www.africa50.com/.

33. Paul Jarvis, interview with Africa50 CEO Alain Ebobissé, Africa50, June 1, 2017, https://www.partnershipsbulletin.com/people/raising-africa.

34. "African Development Bank Unveils Ambitious Electrification Plans 'Because Africans Are Tired of Being in the Dark,'" *Why Electricity Matters*, May 5, 2017.

35. "Power Africa Launches New Initiative at African Utility Week," Power Africa, May 18, 2017.

36. *IBM Global Commuter Pain Survey: Traffic Congestion Down*, IBM, September 2011.

37. Bughin et al., *Lions on the Move II*.

38. Somik Vinay Lall, J. Vernon Henderson, and Anthony J. Venables, *Africa's Cities: Opening Doors to the World*, World Bank, 2017.

39. "Healthcare Is Becoming Big Business in Africa, Albeit Slowly," *Financial Times*, May 10, 2017.

40. Jonathan Wheatley, "Nigeria's 'Great Farm' Model Bears Fruit in Time of High Insecurity," *Financial Times*, November 7, 2017.

41. Ibid.

42. Emiko Terazono, "Japan's Mitsui to Invest in African Food Commodities Trader," *Financial Times*, November 22, 2017.

43. "Agricultural Investment Programmes Boost Production in Morocco," Oxford Business Group, 2015, https://oxfordbusinessgroup.com/overview/agricultural-investment-programmes-boost-production-morocco.

44. Acha Leke et al., *South Africa's Big Five*.

45. Reuters staff, "Eni and Anadarko Join Forces on Mozambique Gas Projects," *Reuters*, December 3, 2015.

46. Borges Nhamire and Paul Burkhardt, "Eni Finalizes $7 Billion Mozambique Gas Project Investment," *Bloomberg*, June 2, 2017.

47. Scott Desmarais and Marc Stoneham, *Rising Up: Unlocking the Potential of Africa's Oil and Gas*, McKinsey & Company, December 2014.

48. Collier, *The Plundered Planet*.

49. Neil Hume, "Gem Diamonds up 15% on 910 Carat Diamond Find," *Financial Times*, January 15, 2018.

50. Mia Breytenbach, "Sula to Pursue DRC Cobalt Opportunities as It Changes Name to African Battery Metals," *Creamer Media's Mining Weekly*, January 18, 2018.

51. "OCP Reports Earnings for Fourth Quarter and Full Year 2016," OCP, March 2017.

52. Akash Dowra et al., *Creating Global Mining Winners in Africa*, McKinsey & Company, February 2016.

53. *Sustainability Report 2014*, Randgold Resources, http://www.randgoldresources.com/files/sustainability-report-2014.

54. James Manyika and Charles Roxburgh, *The Great Transformer: The Impact of the Internet on Economic Growth and Prosperity*, McKinsey Global Institute, October 2011.

55. James Manyika et al., *Lions Go Digital: The Internet's Transformative Potential in Africa*, McKinsey Global Institute, November 2013, https://www.mckinsey.com/industries/high-tech/our-insights/lions-go-digital-the-internets-transformative-potential-in-africa.

56. Manyika and Roxburgh, *The Great Transformer*.

57. Analysys Mason DataHub, http://www.analysysmason.com/services/Research/DataHub/.

58. Figures based on McKinsey analysis of data from Analysys Mason (http://www.analysysmason.com).

59. Ibid.

60. Euromonitor International, 2016, from trade sources and national statistics.

61. Mutsa Chironga, Hilary De Grandis, and Yassir Zouaoui, *Mobile Financial Services in Africa: Winning the Battle for the Customer*, McKinsey & Company, September 2017.

CHAPTER 3

1. "Saham Group Becomes a Pan-African Investment Fund and Sells Its Insurance Business to Sanlam," *BusinessWire*, March 8, 2018.

2. Jacques Bughin et al., *Lions on the Move II: Realizing the Potential of Africa's Economies*, McKinsey Global Institute, September 2016.

3. Mutsa Chironga et al., *Roaring to Life*: *Growth and Innovation in African Retail Banking*, McKinsey & Company, February 2018.

4. Elena Holodny, "The 13 Fastest-Growing Economies in the World," *Business Insider*, June 12, 2015.

5. Robert Muggah and David Kilcullen, "These Are Africa's Fastest-Growing Cities—and They'll Make or Break the Continent," World Economic Forum, May 4, 2016, https://www.weforum.org/agenda/2016/05/africa-biggest-cities-fragility/.

6. Joe Myers, "These Are Africa's Fastest-Growing Cities," *CNBC Africa*, May 25, 2016.

7. Ibid.

8. Maggie Fick, "Coca-Cola Buys Stake in Nigerian Juice and Dairy Company CHI," *Financial Times*, January 30, 2016.

9. Toby Shapshak, "Liquid Telecom to Be Largest Pan-African Broadband Network with Neotel Purchase," *Forbes*, June 28, 2016.

10. "Arla Foods, Tolaram Group Partner to Market Dano Milk," *Beverage Industry News*, November 19, 2015.

11. Dinfin Mulupi, "Informal Retail 'A Market You Can't Afford to Ignore,'" *How We Made It in Africa*, January 12, 2015, https://www.howwemadeitinafrica.com/informal-retail-a-market-you-cant-afford-to-ignore/45983/.

12. Achim Berg et al., *The Apparel Sourcing Caravan's Next Stop: Digitization*, McKinsey & Company, September 2017.

13. Jacques Bughin, Levente Jánoskuti, and András Havas, *The Next Gold Medal: How Hungary Can Win the Productivity Race in the Digital Age*, McKinsey & Company, September 2016; Eduardo Zachary Albrecht and Betty Chemier, "Tanger Med: Renault's Investment in Morocco," *Fair Observer*, July 6, 2014; Elizia Volkmann, "French Connection Nurturing Morocco's Auto Industry," *Wards Auto*, April 12, 2016; Groupe Renault website, https://group.renault.com/en/our-company/locations/our-industrial-locations/tangier-plant/; Tanger Automotive City website, www.tac.ma/.

14. Thomas Farole, *Special Economic Zones in Africa*, World Bank, 2011, https://openknowledge.worldbank.org/handle/10986/2268.

15. Irene Yuan Sun, Kartik Jayaram, and Omid Kassiri, *Dance of the Lions and Dragons: How Are Africa and China Engaging, and How Will the Partnership Evolve?* June 2017.

16. Matina Stevis, "Kenya's Tech Hub Gets a Makeover," *Wall Street Journal*, April 11, 2017.

CHAPTER 4

1. "Kellogg Company and Tolaram Announce New, Long-Term Partnership to Significantly Expand Presence in Africa," press release, September 15, 2015, http://newsroom.kelloggcompany.com/2015-09-15-Kellogg-Company-and-Tolaram-Announce-New-Long-Term-Partnership-to-Significantly-Expand-Presence-in-Africa.

2. Clayton M. Christensen, Efosa Ojomo, and Derek van Bever, "Africa's New Generation of Innovators," *Harvard Business Review*, January–February 2017, 128–136.

3. Equity Bank financial results, 2017, Equity Group Holdings Plc, October 30, 2017. https://www.equitybankgroup.com/investor-relations/financial-results.

4. *Identifying and Capturing Market Opportunity in Africa through Private Sector Innovation: An Introduction to LafargeHolcim Affordable Housing*, Centre for Affordable Housing Finance in Africa, January 6, 2016, http://housingfinanceafrica.org/identifying-and-capturing-market-opportunity-in-africa-through-private-sector-innovation-an-introduction-to-lafargeholcim-affordable-housing/.

5. Irene Yuan Sun, Kartik Jayaram, and Omid Kassiri, *Dance of the Lions and Dragons: How Are Africa and China Engaging, and How Will the Partnership Evolve?* McKinsey & Company, June 2017.

6. "Business in Nigeria: Africa's Testing Ground," *The Economist*, August 23, 2014.

7. Mutsa Chironga et al., *Roaring to Life: Growth and Innovation in African Retail Banking*, McKinsey & Company, February 2018.

8. Ibid.

9. Sun, Jayaram, and Kassiri, *Dance of the Lions and Dragons*.

10. Ibid.

11. Mutsa Chironga, Hilary De Grandis, and Yassir Zouaoui, *Mobile Financial Services in Africa: Winning the Battle for the Customer*, McKinsey & Company, September 2017.

12. Caroline Howard, "EdTech Giant 2U Acquires GetSmarter for $103 Million," *Forbes*, May 2, 2017.

13. Kate Douglas, "How mPedigree Built a Business by Combating Counterfeit Products," *How We Made It in Africa*, August 26, 2015, https://www.howwemadeitinafrica.com/how-mpedigree-built-a-business-by-combating-counterfeit-products/51384/.

14. David Herbling, "Equity Group to Help Open Chain of Health Clinics," *Business Daily*, March 2, 2015.

CHAPTER 5

1. Irene Yuan Sun, Kartik Jayaram, and Omid Kassiri, *Dance of the Lions and Dragons: How Are Africa and China Engaging, and How Will the Partnership Evolve?* McKinsey & Company, June 2017.

2. Dominic Barton, James Manyika, and Sarah Keohane Williamson, "Finally, Evidence That Managing for the Long Term Pays Off," hbr.org, February 7, 2017, https://hbr.org/2017/02/finally-proof-that-managing-for-the-long-term-pays-off.

3. See Jacques Bughin et al., *Lions on the Move II: Realizing the Potential of Africa's Economies*, McKinsey Global Institute, September 2016.

4. "Mohammed Dewji: A Made in Africa Success Story," *African Business Magazine*, January 23, 2017.

5. "Supply Chain Management," Shoprite Holdings Ltd., n.d., https://www.shopriteholdings.co.za/trade-partners/supply-chain-management.html.

6. "Power Africa and Black Rhino Partner to Electrify Africa," Black Rhino, n.d., http://blackrhinogroup.com/power-africa-and-black-rhino/.

7. Africa Ariño, "Strategies That Go the Distance in Africa," *IESE Insight*, first quarter 2015.

8. McKinsey interview with Mohammed Dewji, August 2017.

9. "Mohammed Dewji: A Made in Africa Success Story," *African Business Magazine,* January 23, 2017.

10. Terence McNamee, Mark Pearson, and Wiebe Boer, eds., *Africans Investing in Africa: Understanding Business and Trade, Sector by Sector* (New York: Palgrave Macmillan, 2015).

11. The Ibrahim Index of African Governance (IIAG) is a tool that measures and monitors governance performance in African countries.

12. "International Anti-Corruption Day: AfDB Calls for Stronger Measures in Africa," African Development Bank, December 10, 2015, https://www.afdb.org/en/news-and-events/international-anti-corruption-day-afdb-calls-for-stronger-measures-in-africa-15205/.

13. Caryn Peiffer and Richard Rose, "Why Are the Poor More Vulnerable to Bribery in Africa? The Institutional Effects of Services," *Taylor & Francis*

Online, December 5, 2016, https://www.tandfonline.com/doi/full/10.1080/00220 388.2016.1257121.

14. *People and Corruption: Africa Survey 2015—Global Corruption Barometer*, Transparency International, December 1, 2015, https://www.transparency.org/ whatwedo/publication/people_and_corruption_africa_survey_2015.

CHAPTER 6

1. "Boomtown Slum: A Day in the Economic Life of Africa's Biggest Shanty-Town," *The Economist*, December 22, 2012.

2. *Talent Shortage Survey*, ManpowerGroup, May 2015, https://www .manpowergroup.com/wps/wcm/connect/db23c560-08b6-485f-9bf6-f5f38a43c76a/2015_Talent_Shortage_Survey_US-lo_res.pdf?MOD=AJPERES.

3. The OECD measures this phenomenon by country. In Africa there are a large number of countries where more than 20 percent of the university graduates live in an OECD country, and few with less than 5 percent.

4. David Fine et al., *Africa at Work: Job Creation and Inclusive Growth*, McKinsey Global Institute, August 2012.

5. Irene Yuan Sun, Kartik Jayaram, and Omid Kassiri, *Dance of the Lions and Dragons: How Are Africa and China Engaging, and How Will the Partnership Evolve?* McKinsey & Company, June 2017.

6. *MTN Group Limited Integrated Report for the Year Ended 31 December 2013*, MTN Group, 2014, http://www.mtn-investor.com/mtn_ar2013/index.php.

7. www.dangotecement.com/careers/dangote-academy/.

8. Lohini Moodley et al., *Women Matter Africa*, McKinsey & Company, August 2016.

9. Georges Desvaux, Sandrine Devillard-Hoellinger, and Pascal Baumgarten, *Women Matter: Gender Diversity, a Corporate Performance Driver*, McKinsey & Company, 2007.

CONCLUSION

1. Hanna Ziady, "CEO Initiative Fund Gears Up to Aid SMEs," *Business Day*, March 26, 2017.

2. See Dominic Barton, "Capitalism for the Long Term," *Harvard Business Review*, March 2011.

3. Nelson Mandela, *Long Walk to Freedom: The Autobiography of Nelson Mandela* (Boston: Back Bay Books, 1995).

SELECTED BIBLIOGRAPHY

Africa50. "Homepage." https://www.africa50.com/.

African Development Bank Group. *Tracking Africa's Progress in Figures*, 2014.

African Library Project. "Africa Literacy Facts." https://www
.africanlibraryproject.org/our-african-libraries/africa-facts.

Andriamananjara, Soamiely. "Understanding the Importance of the Tripartite
Free Trade Area." *Brookings*, June 17, 2015. https://www.brookings.edu/
blog/africa-in-focus/2015/06/17/understanding-the-importance-of-the-
tripartite-free-trade-area/.

Ariño, Africa. "Strategies that Go the Distance in Africa." *IESE Insight* (First
quarter 2015): 24–31.

Barton, Dominic. "Capitalism for the Long Term." *Harvard Business Review*,
March 2011, 84–91.

Barton, Dominic, James Manyika, and Sarah Keohane Williamson. "Finally,
Evidence that Managing for the Long Term Pays Off." *Harvard Business
Review*, February 7, 2017. https://hbr.org/2017/02/finally-proof-that-
managing-for-the-long-term-pays-off.

Berg, Achim, Saskia Hedrich, Tim Lange, and Karl-Hendrick Magnus.
Digitization: The Next Stop for the Apparel Sourcing Caravan. McKinsey &
Company, September 2017. https://www.mckinsey.com/industries/retail/
our-insights/digitization-the-next-stop-for-the-apparel-sourcing-caravan.

Bisson, Peter, Rik Kirkland, and Elizabeth Stephenson. *The Great
Rebalancing*. McKinsey & Company, June 2010. https://www.mckinsey.com/
business-functions/strategy-and-corporate-finance/our-insights/the-great-
rebalancing.

Bradley, Chris, Martin Hirt, and Sven Smit. *Strategy Beyond the Hockey Stick:
People, Probabilities, and Big Moves to Beat the Odds*. Hoboken, NJ: Wiley. 2018.

Bright, Jake. "An e-Commerce Challenge in Africa: Selling to People Who
Aren't Online." *The New Yorker,* June 30, 2016.

Bughin, Jacques, Mutsa Chironga, Georges Desvaux, Tenbite Ermias, Paul
Jacobson, Omid Kassiri, Acha Leke, Susan Lund, Arend van Wamelen, and
Yassir Zouaoui. *Lions on the Move II: Realizing the Potential of Africa's
Economies*. McKinsey Global Institute, September 2016. https://www
.mckinsey.com/global-themes/middle-east-and-africa/lions-on-the-move-
realizing-the-potential-of-africas-economies.

Bughin, Jacques, Levente Jánoskuti, and András Havas. *The Next Gold Medal: How Hungary Can Win the Productivity Race in the Digital Age.* McKinsey & Company, September 2016. https://www.mckinsey.com/global-themes/ europe/the-next-gold-medal-how-hungary-can-win-the-productivity-race-in-the-digital-age.

Castellano, Antonio, Adam Kendall, Mikhail Nikomarov, and Tarryn Swemmer. *Brighter Africa: The Growth Potential of the Sub-Saharan Electricity Sector.* McKinsey & Company, February 2015. https://www .icafrica.org/fileadmin/documents/Knowledge/Energy/McKensey-Brighter_ Africa_The_growth_potential_of_the_sub-Saharan_electricity_sector.pdf.

Chironga, Mutsa, Luis Cunha, Hilary De Grandis, and Mayowa Kuyor. *Roaring to Life: Growth and Innovation in African Retail Banking.* McKinsey & Company, February 2018. https://www.mckinsey.com/~/media/ McKinsey/Industries/Financial%20Services/Our%20Insights/African%20 retail%20bankings%20next%20growth%20frontier/Roaring-to-life-growth-and-innovation-in-African-retail-banking-web-final.ashx.

Chironga, Mutsa, Hilary De Grandis, and Yassir Zouaoui. *Mobile Financial Services in Africa: Winning the Battle for the Customer.* McKinsey & Company, September 2017. https://www.mckinsey.com/industries/financial-services/our-insights/mobile-financial-services-in-africa-winning-the-battle-for-the-customer.

Christensen, Clayton M., Efosa Ojomo, and Derek van Bever. "Africa's New Generation of Innovators." *Harvard Business Review*, January–February 2017, 128–136.

Collier, Paul. *African Urbanization: An Analytic Policy Guide.* Working Paper. London: International Growth Centre, 2016.

Collier, Paul. *The Plundered Planet: How to Reconcile Prosperity with Nature.* New York: Oxford University Press, 2010.

Dobbs, Richard, Yougang Chen, Gordon Orr, James Manyika, Michael Chui, and Elsie Chang. *China's e-Tail Revolution: Online Shopping as a Catalyst for Growth.* McKinsey Global Institute, March 2013. https://www.mckinsey .com/global-themes/asia-pacific/china-e-tailing.

Dobbs, Richard, Herbert Pohl, Diaan-Yi Lin, Jan Mischke, Nicklas Garemo, Jimmy Hexter, Stefan Matzinger, Robert Palter, and Rushad Nanavatty. *Infrastructure Productivity: How to Save $1 Trillion a Year.* McKinsey Global Institute, January 2013. https://www.mckinsey.com/industries/capital-projects-and-infrastructure/our-insights/infrastructure-productivity.

du Rausas, Matthieu Pélissié, James Manyika, Eric Hazan, Jacques Bughin, Michael Chui, and Rémi Said. *Internet Matters: The Net's Sweeping Impact on Growth, Jobs, and Prosperity.* McKinsey Global Institute, May 2011. https://www.mckinsey.com/industries/high-tech/our-insights/ internet-matters.

The Economist. "Boomtown Slum: A Day in the Economic Life of Africa's Biggest Shanty-Town," December 22, 2012.

The Economist. "Business in Nigeria: Africa's Testing Ground," August 23, 2014.

Ekekwe, Ndubuisi. "How Digital Technology Is Changing Farming in Africa." *Harvard Business Review*, May 18, 2017. https://hbr.org/2017/05/how-digital-technology-is-changing-farming-in-africa.

Farole, Thomas. *Special Economic Zones in Africa.* World Bank, 2011.

Feser, Claudio, Fernanda Mayol, and Ramesh Srinivasan. "Decoding Leadership: What Really Matters." *The McKinsey Quarterly*, January 2015.

Fine, David, Arend van Wamelen, Susan Lund, Armando Cabral, Mourad Taoufiki, Norbert Dörr, Acha Leke, Charles Roxburgh, Jörg Schubert, and Paul Cook. *Africa at Work: Job Creation and Inclusive Growth.* McKinsey Global Institute, August 2012. https://www.mckinsey.com/global-themes/middle-east-and-africa/africa-at-work.

Gelb, Alan, Christian Meyer, Vijaya Ramachandran, and Divyanshi Wadhwa. "Can Africa Be a Manufacturing Destination? Labor Costs in Comparative Perspective." Center for Global Development, October 2017.

Greenberg, Ezra, Martin Hirt, and Sven Smit, "The Global Forces Inspiring a New Narrative of Progress," *The McKinsey Quarterly*, April 2017.

Hattingh, Damian, Acha Leke, and Bill Russo. *Lions (Still) on the Move: Growth in Africa's Consumer Sector.* McKinsey Global Institute, October 2017. https://www.mckinsey.com/industries/consumer-packaged-goods/our-insights/lions-still-on-the-move-growth-in-africas-consumer-sector.

Holt, Tania, Medhi Lahrichi, and Jorge Santos de Silva. *Africa: A Continent of Opportunity for Pharma and Patients.* McKinsey & Company, June 2015. https://www.mckinsey.com/industries/pharmaceuticals-and-medical-products/our-insights/africa-a-continent-of-opportunity-for-pharma-and-patients.

Infrastructure Consortium for Africa. *Infrastructure Financing Trends in Africa: ICA Annual Report 2014.* (2015). https://www.icafrica.org/fileadmin/documents/Annual_Reports/INFRASTRUCTURE_FINANCING_TRENDS_IN_AFRICA_%E2%80%93_2014.pdf.

International Monetary Fund. *Regional Economic Outlook Reports (REO), May 2017,* 2017. http://datahelp.imf.org/knowledgebase/articles/500086-regional-economic-outlook-reports-reo.

Jones, C. I. "The Facts of Economic Growth." *Handbook of Macroeconomics,* vol. 2A. Amsterdam: Elsevier B.V., 2016.

Juma, Calestous, and Francis Mangeni. "The Benefits of Africa's New Free Trade Area." Harvard Kennedy School Belfer Center for Science and International Affairs, June 11, 2015.

Kendall, Jake, Robert Schiff, and Emmanuel Smadja. *Sub-Saharan Africa: A Major Potential Revenue Opportunity for Digital Payments.* McKinsey & Company, February 2014. https://www.mckinsey.com/industries/financial-services/our-insights/sub-saharan-africa-a-major-potential-revenue-opportunity-for-digital-payments.

Lacqua, Francine. "Africa's Richest Man Has a Plan: Cement, then Oil—then Arsenal FC." *Bloomberg Markets,* August 17, 2017.

Lala, Ajay, Mukani Moyo, Stefan Rehbach, and Richard Sellschop. *Productivity in Mining Operations: Reversing the Downward Trend.* McKinsey & Company, May 2015.

Lall, Somik Vinay, J. Vernon Henderson, and Anthony J. Venables. *Africa's Cities: Opening Doors to the World*. World Bank, 2017.

Leke, Acha, David Fine, Richard Dobbs, Nomfanelo Magwentshu, Susan Lund, Christine Wu, and Paul Jacobson. *South Africa's Big Five: Bold Priorities for Inclusive Growth*. McKinsey Global Institute, August 2015. https://www.mckinsey.com/global-themes/middle-east-and-africa/south-africas-bold-priorities-for-inclusive-growth.

Leke, Acha, Reinaldo Fiorini, Richard Dobbs, Fraser Thompson, Aliyu Suleiman, and David Wright. *Nigeria's Renewal: Delivering Inclusive Growth in Africa's Largest Economy*. McKinsey Global Institute, July 2014. https://www.mckinsey.com/global-themes/middle-east-and-africa/nigerias-renewal-delivering-inclusive-growth.

Mandela, Nelson. *Long Walk to Freedom: The Autobiography of Nelson Mandela*. Boston: Back Bay Books, 1995.

Manyika, James, Armando Cabral, Lohini Moodley, Suraj Moraje, Safroadu Yeboah-Amankwah, Michael Chui, and Jerry Anthonyrajah. *Lions Go Digital: The Internet's Transformative Potential in Africa*. McKinsey Global Institute, November 2013. https://www.mckinsey.com/industries/high-tech/our-insights/lions-go-digital-the-internets-transformative-potential-in-africa.

Manyika, James, Michael Chui, Jacques Bughin, Richard Dobbs, Peter Bisson, and Alex Marrs. *Disruptive Technologies: Advances that Will Transform Life, Business, and the Global Economy*. McKinsey Global Institute, May 2013. https://www.mckinsey.com/business-functions/digital-mckinsey/our-insights/disruptive-technologies.

Manyika, James, Susan Lund, Marc Singer, Olivia White, and Chris Berry. *Digital Finance for All: Powering Inclusive Growth in Emerging Economies*. McKinsey Global Institute, September 2016. https://www.mckinsey.com/~/media/McKinsey/Global%20Themes/Employment%20and%20Growth/How%20digital%20finance%20could%20boost%20growth%20in%20emerging%20economies/MGI-Digital-Finance-For-All-Executive-summary-September-2016.ashx.

McKinsey & Company (eds.). *Reimagining South Africa: 20 Reflections by Leaders from South Africa and Beyond*. Johannesburg, 2015.

McNamee, Terence, Mark Pearson, and Wiebe Boer, eds. *Africans Investing in Africa: Understanding Business and Trade, Sector by Sector*. Basingstoke, UK: Palgrave Macmillan, 2015.

Medina, Leandro, Andrew W. Jonelis, and Mehmet Cangul. *The Informal Economy in Sub-Saharan Africa*, IMF Working Paper Number 17/156. Washington, DC: International Monetary Fund, July 2017.

Mo Ibrahim Foundation. *A Decade of African Governance 2006–2015*. Mo Ibrahim Foundation, 2016.

Moodley, Lohini, Tania Holt, Acha Leke, and Georges Desvaux. *Women Matter Africa: Making Gender Diversity a Reality*. McKinsey & Company, August 2016. https://www.mckinsey.com/global-themes/gender-equality/women-matter-africa.

Muggah, Robert, and David Kilcullen. "These Are Africa's Fastest-Growing Cities—and They'll Make or Break the Continent." *World Economic Forum*, May 4, 2016.

Mulupi, Dinfin. "Informal Retail 'a Market You Can't Afford to Ignore.'" *How We Made It in Africa*, January 12, 2015.

Pring, Coralie. "People and Corruption: Africa Survey 2015—Global Corruption Barometer." Transparency International, December 1, 2015. https://www.transparency.org/whatwedo/publication/people_and_corruption_africa_survey_2015.

Roxburgh, Charles, Norbert Dörr, Acha Leke, Amine Tazi-Riffi, Arend van Wamelan, Susan Lund, Mutsa Chironga, Tarik Alatovik, Charles Atkins, Nadia Terfous, and Till Zeino-Mahmalat. *Lions on the Move: The Progress and Potential of African Economies*. McKinsey Global Institute, June 2010. https://www.mckinsey.com/global-themes/middle-east-and-africa/lions-on-the-move.

Sun, Irene Yuan. *The Next Factory of the World: How Chinese Investment Is Reshaping Africa*. Boston: Harvard Business Review Press, 2017.

Sun, Irene Yuan. "The World's Next Great Manufacturing Center." *Harvard Business Review*, May–June 2017, 122–129.

Sun, Irene Yuan, Kartik Jayaram, and Omid Kassiri. *Dance of the Lions and Dragons: How Are Africa and China Engaging, and How Will the Partnership Evolve?* McKinsey & Company, June 2017. https://www.mckinsey.com/~/media/McKinsey/Global%20Themes/Middle%20East%20and%20Africa/The%20closest%20look%20yet%20at%20Chinese%20economic%20engagement%20in%20Africa/Dance-of-the-lions-and-dragons.ashx.

Thakkar, Ashish J. *The Lion Awakes: Adventures in Africa's Economic Miracle*. Basingstoke, UK: Palgrave Macmillan, 2015.

United Nations Development Programme. *Africa Human Development Report 2016: Accelerating Gender Equality and Women's Empowerment in Africa*, August 2016. http://www.undp.org/content/undp/en/home/librarypage/hdr/2016-africa-human-development-report.html.

White, David, Mehrdad Baghai, and Stephen Coley. *The Alchemy of Growth*. Hoboken, NJ: Wiley, 1999.

World Bank. *Doing Business 2018: Reforming to Create Jobs*, October 31, 2017. http://www.doingbusiness.org/~/media/WBG/DoingBusiness/Documents/Annual-Reports/English/DB2018-Full-Report.pdf.

World Bank. *Global Economic Prospects: A Fragile Recovery: June 2017*. https://openknowledge.worldbank.org/bitstream/handle/10986/26800/9781464810244.pdf.

World Bank. "While Poverty in Africa Has Declined, Number of Poor Has Increased." *Poverty in a Rising Africa: Africa Poverty Report,* March 2016. http://www.worldbank.org/en/region/afr/publication/poverty-rising-africa-poverty-report.

INDEX

ACKNOWLEDGMENTS

First and foremost, thank you to the many CEOs, executives, and leaders of development institutions who generously shared their experience and insights on business-building in Africa—along with their passion for the continent. This book is infinitely richer for their contributions. They include Akinwumi Adesina, President, African Development Bank; Kofo Akinkugbe, CEO, SecureID; Jean-Louis Billon, former CEO, SIFCA; Mark Bowman, former Managing Director, Africa region, SABMiller; Alex Brand, Director of Operations, Liberty Eagle Kenya Limited; Manu Chandaria, Chairman, Comcraft Group; Gilbert Cheruiyot, Chief Executive, Gilchery Skip-Trace; Paul Collier, Professor of Economics and Public Policy, Blavatnik School of Government, Oxford University; Alex Cummings, former President, Africa Group, and Chief Administrative Officer, Coca-Cola; Aliko Dangote, President and Chief Executive, Dangote Industries Limited; Mohammed Dewji, Managing Director and CEO, MeTL; Mitchell Elegbe, CEO, Interswitch; Tony Elumelu, Chairman, Heirs Holdings and United Bank for Africa, and founder of the Tony Elumelu Foundation; Nadia Fettah, CEO, Saham Finances; Huang Shiyi, Chief Strategy & Investment Officer, CGCOC Group; Jay Ireland, President and CEO, GE Africa; Donald Kaberuka, former President, African Development Bank; Graça Machel, Chair, Graça Machel Trust; Strive Masiyiwa, Executive Chairman, Econet Group;

Dan Matjila, CEO, Public Investment Corporation; Sara Menker, CEO, Gro Intelligence; Phumzile Mlambo-Ngcuka, Executive Director, UN Women; Jesse Moore, CEO, M-Kopa; James Mwangi, Managing Director and CEO, Equity Group Holdings; Nicky Newton-King, CEO, Johannesburg Stock Exchange; Ngozi Okonjo-Iweala, former Minister of Finance, Nigeria; Tayo Oviosu, CEO, Paga; Sacha Poignonnec, Co-CEO, Jumia; Patrick Pouyanné, Chairman and CEO, Total; Deepak Singhal, CEO, Dufil Prima Foods; Vera Songwe, Executive Secretary, United Nations Economic Commission for Africa; Fred Swaniker, cofounder, African Leadership Group; Ashish J. Thakkar, founder, Mara Group; Tidjane Thiam, CEO, Credit Suisse; Danladi Verheijen, Managing Director, Verod Capital Management; Brooks Washington, founder and Principal, Roha. We also thank the more than one thousand executives from across the world who participated in our Africa business survey, a key data source for the book.

McKinsey & Company exists to help its clients make distinctive, lasting, and substantial improvements in their performance—and many of the insights we share in this book have been honed through our work in shaping strategy and transforming operations and organizations for our clients across Africa. We thank the management teams of every one of our clients for the opportunity to be part of your African growth stories.

Although there are three authors listed on the cover of this book, the thinking behind it is the fruit of a much bigger team. We thank our partners in McKinsey's African offices—and beyond—for believing in this project, backing it with such enthusiasm, sharing their insights and networks, and participating in many of the interviews conducted for the book. Particular thanks go to Yaw Agyenim-Boateng, Jalil Bensouda, Jon Cummings, Damian Hattingh, Tania Holt, Kartik Jayaram,

Omid Kassiri, Adam Kendall, Kannan Lakmeeharan, James Manyika, Lohini Moodley, Bill Russo, and Saf Yeboah-Amankwah. We also thank our coauthors of the McKinsey Global Institute's *Lions on the Move* reports, which provided the initial research base on which the book was built.

We also benefited from the incredible dedication and creative thinking of a core team of McKinsey colleagues who brainstormed approaches, conducted fresh analysis, and managed complex logistics. They included Rik Kirkland, partner in charge of McKinsey's global publishing, and a team of Africa-based consultants and specialists led by Hilda Kragha and Desh Pillay and including Saad El Mansouri, Tayo Emden, Adeyemi Gafaar, Tarryn Govender, Khanya Gwaza, Boye Jesse, Lungelo Mnguni, Niyi Ogunbayo, Sidhika Ramlakan, Ekemezie Uche, and Roshni Walia. We also thank Heather Hanselman and Daniella Seiler of McKinsey Insights, who designed and orchestrated our Africa business survey with great creativity and professionalism. Many other McKinsey colleagues provided ideas, advice, and practical help. Three who stand out are Amandla Ooko-Ombaka, Philip Osafo-Kwaako, and Fransje Van Der Marel.

Writing a book such as this requires both art and science. For the artistry, we are indebted to Colin Douglas and Mary Kuntz, whose elegant writing and editing contributed enormously to the final shape of the book. Melinda Merino helped shape the idea for the book and was a passionate, incisive companion throughout the writing journey. She and her dedicated colleagues at Harvard Business Review Press could not have been better partners. McKinsey's editorial production team carefully reviewed and fact-checked the entire manuscript; its members include Gwyn Herbein, Dana Sand, Venetia Simcock, Katie Turner, Sneha Vats, Pooja Yadav, and Belinda Yu.

Last but not least, we thank the entrepreneurs and business executives from across Africa and the world who are thinking big, taking risks, and innovating to provide better products, services, and solutions for Africa's people. You are the true leaders of Africa's business revolution.

ABOUT THE AUTHORS

ACHA LEKE is a senior partner at McKinsey & Company and chairman of its Africa practice. He is based in Johannesburg. Acha joined McKinsey in 1999, went on to establish the firm's Nigeria office in 2010, and has been at the forefront of McKinsey's expansion across Africa, working in more than twenty countries. His leadership roles at McKinsey include senior partner in charge of global recruiting and council member of the McKinsey Global Institute (MGI). Acha is motivated by one overarching question: "Will it have mattered to Africa that I lived?" This prompted him to cofound the African Leadership Group, which includes the African Leadership Academy and the African Leadership Network. He has worked to ease travel restrictions in Africa, which has led many countries to drop visa requirements for fellow Africans, and serves on a committee to reform the African Union, chaired by President Paul Kagame of Rwanda. Acha has received many awards and recognitions, has authored dozens of articles for publications including *Harvard Business Review* and the *McKinsey Quarterly*, and is coauthor of MGI's widely recognized *Lions on the Move* reports on the progress and potential of Africa's economies.

MUTSA CHIRONGA is divisional executive for consumer banking at Nedbank, one of South Africa's largest banking groups, where his focus is on growing the customer base and deepening relationships with more than seven million existing customers. Mutsa was previously a partner at McKinsey & Company, based in Johannesburg. In that role he worked with banks in more than a dozen African countries on topics including strategy, expansion across the African continent, and performance transformation. Mutsa is an Archbishop Desmond Tutu Leadership Fellow, one of approximately two hundred young leaders from across Africa. He has published widely. He was lead author of the McKinsey reports *Roaring to Life: Growth and Innovation in African Retail Banking* and *Mobile Financial Services in Africa: Winning the Battle for the Customer*. With Acha Leke, he coauthored the McKinsey Global Institute's *Lions on the Move* reports on Africa's economies.

GEORGES DESVAUX is a senior partner at McKinsey & Company, a former managing partner of the firm's African and Japanese offices, and a member of McKinsey's shareholders' council, the firm's governing body. In his three decades with McKinsey he has been based in Brussels, Paris, Beijing, Tokyo, and Johannesburg. He is now based in Hong Kong, where his focus includes advising Asian companies on their African expansion strategies. Georges has supported retailers, financial institutions, and technology companies on international growth, postmerger integration, marketing, operations, and organizational design. As a leader of McKinsey's global marketing practice, he has helped build the firm's consumer insights and analytics capabilities and has coauthored numerous reports and articles on consumer and macroeconomic trends— including the MGI report *Lions on the Move II: Realizing the Potential of Africa's Economies*. Since 2007, Georges has co-led McKinsey's *Women Matter* research initiative on women's advancement in business. He has coauthored several reports and articles on the topic, including *Women Matter Africa*.